Quotations
for Speakers

Quotations for Speakers

NORMAN WEED

DAVID & CHARLES
Newton Abbot   London   North Pomfret (Vt)

British Library Cataloguing in Publication Data

Quotations for speakers.
1. Quotations, English
I. Weed, Norman
808.88'2   PN6081

ISBN 0–7153–8111–3

Library of Congress Catalog Card Number 80–70295

Typeset by Typesetters (Birmingham) Limited,
Smethwick, Warley, West Midlands
and printed in Great Britain
by Biddles Limited, Guildford, Surrey
for David & Charles (Publishers) Limited
Brunel House   Newton Abbot   Devon

Published in the United States of America
by David & Charles Inc
North Pomfret   Vermont 05053   USA

Ability: There is something rarer than ability. It is the ability to recognize ability. ELBERT HUBBARD

The superior man is distressed by the limitations of his ability; he is not distressed by the fact that men do not recognize the ability he has. CONFUCIUS

No one knows what he can't do until he tries. ANON

Abscond: To 'move' in a mysterious way, commonly with the property of another. AMBROSE BIERCE

Absolution: God will forgive me; that's HIS business. HEINRICH HEINE

If I owe Smith ten dollars, and God forgives me, that doesn't pay Smith. R. G. INGERSOLL

Abstainer: Abstainer. A weak person, who yields to the temptation of denying himself a pleasure. AMBROSE BIERCE

The dipsomaniac and the abstainer are not only both mistaken, but they both make the same mistake. They both regard wine as a drug and not a drink. G. K. CHESTERTON

Absurdity: A statement or belief manifestly inconsistent with one's own opinion. AMBROSE BIERCE

Accomplishments: You can get almost everything accomplished if you don't mind who gets the credit. NED HAY

Achievement: The world is moving so fast these days that the man who says it can't be done is generally interrupted by somebody doing it. ELBERT HUBBARD

Acquaintance: Acquaintance. A person whom we know well enough to borrow from, but not well enough to lend to. AMBROSE BIERCE

Act of God: An act of God was defined as something which no reasonable man could have expected. SIR A. P. HERBERT

Action: There are three ways to get something done: do it yourself, hire someone, or forbid your kids to do it. ANON

Actor: A man never knows what a fool he is until he hears himself imitated by one. SIR HERBERT BEERBOHM TREE

Admiration. Our polite recognition of another's resemblance to ourselves. AMBROSE BIERCE

Adultery: What men call gallantry, and Gods adultery,
Is much more common when the climate's sultry.
LORD BYRON

Adversary: Treating your adversary with respect is giving him an advantage to which he is not entitled. SAMUEL JOHNSON

Nothing ever perplexes an adversary so much as an appeal to his honour. BENJAMIN DISRAELI

Adversity: There is no one less fortunate than he whom adversity neglects; he has no chance to prove himself. ANON

Advertising: Don't advertise; tell it to a gossip. ANON

Advice: Do not do unto others as you would they should do unto you. Their tastes may not be the same. GEORGE BERNARD SHAW

Only put off until tomorrow what you are willing to die having left undone. PABLO PICASSO

Smart is when you believe only half of what you hear. Brilliant is when you know which half to believe. ANON

Write injuries in dust, benefits in marble. BENJAMIN FRANKLIN

In those days he was wiser than he is now; he used frequently to take my advice. SIR WINSTON CHURCHILL

You will always stay young if you live honestly, eat slowly, sleep sufficiently, work industriously, worship faithfully, and lie about your age. ANON

To ease another's heartache is to forget one's own. ABRAHAM LINCOLN

We all admire the wisdom of people who come to us for advice. ANON

My father when I was young, said, 'Reuben my boy when you grow up, get land. God has stopped making land, but he keeps right on making people.' ANON

It is better to light a candle than to curse the darkness. ANON

When you give honest advice, have one foot out of the door. ANON

If your spirits are low, do something; if you have been doing something, do something different. ANON

Let not thy will roar, when thy power can but whisper. ANON

Always judge a person by the way he treats somebody who can be of no use to him. ANON

Work is the greatest thing in the world, so we should save some of it for tomorrow. ANON

Advise: I advise thee to visit thy relations and friends; but I advise thee not to live too near to them. THOMAS FULLER

Afterthoughts: He is a wise man who has his afterthoughts first. ANON

Age: I am not young enough to know everything. SIR J. M. BARRIE

When men grow virtuous in their old age, they only make a sacrifice to God of the devil's leavings. ALEXANDER POPE

I prefer old age to the alternative. MAURICE CHEVALIER

One compensation of old age is that it excuses you from picnics. WILLIAM FEATHER

It is only in going uphill that one realizes how fast one is going downhill. GEORGE DU MAURIER

The principal objection to old age is that there's no future in it. ANON

You are getting old when the gleam in your eyes is from the sun hitting your bi-focals. ANON

It's a sign of age if you feel like the day after the night before and you haven't been anywhere. ANON

Men of age object too much, consult too long, adventure too little, repent too soon. FRANCIS BACON

As we grow old, the beauty steals inward. RALPH WALDO EMERSON

Age. That period of life in which we compound for the vices that remain by reviling those we have no longer the vigor to commit. AMBROSE BIERCE

The years that a woman subtracts from her age are not lost. They are added to the ages of other women. DIANE DE POLITIERS

Ailments: Why doesn't medical science work out some way to make our ailments as interesting to others as they are to us? ANON

Alcohol: Malt does more than Milton can
    To justify God's ways to man. A. E. HOUSMAN

Ale, man, ale's the stuff to drink
For fellows whom it hurts to think. A. E. HOUSMAN

Alcohol. A liquid for preserving almost everything but secrets. ANON

Alimony: You never realize how short a month is until you pay alimony. JOHN BARRYMORE

Allocation: The same people who can deny others everything are famous for refusing themselves nothing. AMBROSE BIERCE

Ambidextrous: Means being clumsy with both hands. GENE HARDISON

Ambition: Ambition is pitiless. Any merit that it cannot use it finds despicable. JOSEPH JOUBERT

You aim for the palace and get drowned in the sewer. MARK TWAIN

There is a profound causal relation between the height of a man's ambition and the depths of his possible fall. ANON

All competent men should have some ambition, for ambition is like the temper in steel. If there's too much the product is brittle, if there's too little the steel is soft; and without a certain amount of hardness a man cannot achieve what he sets out to do. DWIGHT D. EISENHOWER

America: Americans have a disease which has led them to believe that all they need is their father's money and their mother's charm. ALEXANDER KING

Perhaps after all America has never been discovered. I myself would merely say that it has been detected. OSCAR WILDE

Anonymous: After Shakespeare, the world's most prolific writer of quotations was 'Anon'.

Antique (Collector):
The idiot who praises with enthusiastic tone;
All centuries but this, and every country but his own.
SIR W. S. GILBERT

Apologies: It is mighty presumptuous on your part to suppose your small failures of so much consequence that you must talk about them. DR OLIVER WENDELL HOLMES

Apologist: And finds with keen discriminating sight,
Black's not so black — nor white so very white.
GEORGE CANNING

A stiff apology is a second insult. G. K. CHESTERTON

Apparel: I hold that gentlemen to be the best dressed whose dress no one observes. ANTHONY TROLLOPE

Appeal: In law, to put the dice into the box for another throw. AMBROSE BIERCE

Appetizers: Are little things you keep eating until you lose your appetite. RICHARD ARMOUR

Applause: Do not trust to the cheering, for those very persons would shout as much if you and I were going to be hanged. OLIVER CROMWELL

Appreciation: If you wish to have it good, you must never take anything for granted. SHIRLEY M. DEVER

Architect: No person who is not a great sculptor or painter can be an architect. If he is not a sculptor or painter, he can only be a builder. JOHN RUSKIN

Architecture: Is the art of how to waste space. PHILIP JOHNSON
No architecture is so haughty as that which is simple. JOHN RUSKIN

Arguers: They never open their mouths without subtracting from the sum of human knowledge. SPEAKER THOMAS BRACKET REED

Argument: You have not converted a man because you have silenced him. C. MORLEY

In any argument the man with the greater intelligence is always wrong, because he did not use his intelligence to avoid the argument in the first place. ANON

When you have no basis for an argument, abuse the plaintiff. CICERO

Arguments are to be avoided: they are always vulgar and often convincing. OSCAR WILDE

What's the use of wasting dynamite when insect-powder will do? CARTER GLASS

You raise your voice when you should reinforce your argument. SAMUEL JOHNSON

Arithmetic: That arithmetic is the basest of all mental activities is proved by the fact that it is the only one that can be accomplished by a machine. ARTHUR SCHOPENHAUER

Arrogance: If I cannot brag of knowing something, then I brag of not knowing it; at any rate brag. RALPH WALDO EMERSON

Not to know me argues yourself unknown. JOHN MILTON

Art: There are painters who transform the sun into a yellow spot, but there are others who, thanks to their art and intelligence, transform a yellow spot into the sun. PABLO PICASSO

Any fool can paint a picture, but it takes a wise man to be able to sell it. SAMUEL BUTLER

What is a work of art? A word made flesh . . . a thing seen, or a thing known, the immeasurable translated into terms of the measurable. ERIC GILL

To say of a picture, as is often said in its praise, that it shows great and earnest labour, is to say that it is incomplete and unfit for view. J. M. WHISTLER

Art consists of limitation. The most beautiful part of every picture is the frame. G. K. CHESTERTON

You use a glass mirror to see your face; you use works of art to see your soul. GEORGE BERNARD SHAW

To say that a work of art is good, but incomprehensible to the majority of men, is the same as saying of some kind of food that it is very good but that most people can't eat it. LEO TOLSTOY

Art is a jealous mistress, and if a man has a genius for painting, poetry, music, architecture or philosophy, he makes a bad husband and an ill provider. RALPH WALDO EMERSON

Art is man added to nature. FRANCIS BACON

Artist: Artists do not prove things. They do not need to. They know them. GEORGE BERNARD SHAW

An artist must know how to convince others of the truth of his lies. PABLO PICASSO

His work was that curious mixture of bad painting and good intentions that always entitles a man to be called a representative British artist. OSCAR WILDE

All the arts in America are a gigantic racket run by unscrupulous men for unhealthy women. SIR THOMAS BEECHAM

The English public takes no interest in a work of art until it is told that the work in question is immoral. OSCAR WILDE

For art comes to you, proposing frankly to give nothing but the highest quality to your moments as they pass, and simply for those moments' sake. WALTER PATER

Assassination: Assassination is the extreme form of censorship. GEORGE BERNARD SHAW

Atheism: The least one can ask atheists is not to make their atheism an article of faith. AURELIAN SCHOLL

Nobody talks so constantly about God as those who insist that there is no God. HEYWOOD BROUN

An Irish atheist is one who wishes to God he could believe in God. ANON

Author: Though by whim, envy, or resentment led,
They damn those authors whom they never read.
CHARLES CHURCHILL

There is probably no hell for authors in the next world — they suffer so much from critics and publishers in this. C. N. BOVEE

Authors are judged by strange capricious rules. The great ones are thought mad, the small ones fools. ALEXANDER POPE

No author is a man of genius to his publisher. HEINRICH HEINE

Your manuscript is both good and original; but the part that is good is not original, and the part that is original is not good. SAMUEL JOHNSON

There are three difficulties in authorship: to write anything worth publishing, to find honest men to publish it, and to get sensible men to read it. CHARLES COLTON

What I like in a good author is not what he says, but what he whispers. LOGAN PEARSALL SMITH

What no wife of a writer can ever understand is that a writer is working when he's staring out of the window. BURTON RASCOE

Autobiography: Autobiography is now as common as adultery and hardly less reprehensible. JOHN GRIGG

Autobiography is an unrivalled vehicle for telling the truth about other people. PHILLIP GUEDALLA

Baby: A loud noise at one end and no sense of responsibility at the other. FATHER DONALD KNOX

Every baby born into the world is a finer one than the last. CHARLES DICKENS

Bachelor: When a guy likes to have a ball without a chain, that's a bachelor. ANON

Bachelors know more about women than married men; if they didn't, they'd be married too. H. L. MENCKEN

Backbite: Backbite. To speak of a man as you find him, when he can't find you. AMBROSE BIERCE

Bad taste: What is exhilarating in bad taste is the aristocratic pleasure of giving offence. CHARLES BAUDELAIRE

Bagpipes: Little girl to Scotsman playing bagpipes: 'If you let go, maybe it'll stop screaming.' JAMES UNGER

A bagpipes player, when asked why pipers always walk while they play, explained, 'It's harder to hit a moving target.' ANON

Banking: A banker is a fellow who lends his umbrella when the sun is shining and wants it back the minute it begins to rain. MARK TWAIN

Bargain: It makes no difference what it is, a woman will buy anything she thinks the store is losing money on. KIM HUBBARD

Beauty: Beauty that doesn't make a woman vain makes her very beautiful. JOSH BILLINGS

Biography: A well-written life is almost as rare as a well-spent one. THOMAS CARLYLE

Birth: He that has no fools, knaves, or beggars in his family, was begot by a flash of lightning. ENGLISH PROVERB

Blessed: Is the man who is too busy to worry in the daytime and too sleepy to worry at night. LEO AIKMAN

Blessings: The hardest arithmetic to master is that which enables us to count our blessings. ERIC HOFFER

Bliss: We are never happy: we can only remember that we were so once. ALEXANDER SMITH

Ask yourself whether you are happy, and you cease to be so. JOHN STUART MILL

Bloody Mindedness: A state of mind halfway between anger and cruelty. WAYLAND YOUNG

Bluff: The ability to get to the verge without getting into the war is the necessary art. JOHN FOSTER DULLES

Bluntness: Nine times out of ten, the coarse word is the word that condemns an evil and the refined word the word that excuses it. G. K. CHESTERTON

Book Title: The author who invents a title well,
      Will always find his covered dullness sell.
    THOMAS CHATTERTON

Books: A man's library is a sort of harem. THOMAS A. KEMPIS

Who kills a man kills a reasonable creature, God's image; but he who destroys a good book, kills reason itself, kills the image of God, as it were in the eye. JOHN MILTON

He has left off reading altogether, to the great improvement of his originality. CHARLES LAMB

A good book is the precious life-blood of a master spirit, embalmed and treasured up on purpose to a Life beyond life. JOHN MILTON

Without books God is silent. THOMAS BARTHOLIN

No furniture is as charming as books, even if you never open them. SYDNEY SMITH

The real purpose of books is to trap the mind into doing its own thinking. CHRISTOPHER MARLEY

Bore: Some people are so boring that they make you waste an entire day in five minutes. JULES RENARD

The best way to be boring is to leave nothing out. VOLTAIRE

We often forgive those who bore us, but never those whom we bore. LA ROCHEFOUCAULD

If at first you do succeed, try, try not to be a bore. ANON

Bore. A person who talks when you wish him to listen. AMBROSE BIERCE

A bore is a man who, when you ask him how he is, tells you. BERT LESTON TAYLOR

Boredom: Much of life passes by the bored. ANON

Borrowing: When I lend I am a friend, when I ask I am a foe. SIXTEENTH-CENTURY PROVERB

Boss: When the boss called me an idiot, I agreed. After all, I'm no fool. ANON

Boss to executive assistant: 'Benson, must you concentrate all your imagination, initiative and daring on your expense account?'

Unused power slips imperceptibly into the hands of another. KONRAD HEIDEN

The eye of a master will do more work than both his hands. BENJAMIN FRANKLIN

Boyhood: When you return to your boyhood town, you find it wasn't the town you missed, it was your boyhood. ANON

Brain: Brain. The apparatus with which we think we think. AMBROSE BIERCE

The fundamental cause of trouble in the world today is that the stupid are cocksure while the intelligent are full of doubt. BERTRAND RUSSELL

Breeding: Men are generally more careful of the breed of their horses and dogs than of their children. WILLIAM PENN

Budget: A budget is what you stay within if you go without. ANON

Bulldog-bitch: She is as implacable an adversary as a wife suing for alimony. WILLIAM WYCHERLEY

Bureaucracy: Let us treat men and women well; treat them as if they were real. Perhaps they are. RALPH WALDO EMERSON

If you destroy a free market you create a black market. If you have ten thousand regulations you destroy all respect for the law. SIR WINSTON CHURCHILL

Business: Science may never come up with a better office communication system than the tea break. EARL WILSON

It is well known what a middle-man is; he is a man who bamboozles one party and plunders the other. BENJAMIN DISRAELI

He that resolves to deal with none but honest men must leave off dealing. ENGLISH PROVERB

When you are skinning your customers you should leave some skin on to grow again so that you can skin them again. NIKITA KHRUSHCHEV

An efficiency expert is one who is smart enough to tell you how to run your business and too smart to start one of his own. ANON

Executive to employee: 'I can't approve your expense account Jones, but we'd like to buy the fiction rights to it.'

Secretary on telephone: 'Our automatic answering device is away for repairs – this is a person speaking.'

Do other men, for they would do you; that's the true business precept. CHARLES DICKENS

Buying and Selling: To sell something tell a woman it's a bargain; tell a man its tax deductible. EARL WILSON

Capital Investment: We cannot eat the fruit while the tree is in blossom. BENJAMIN DISRAELI

Capitalism/Socialism: The inherent vice of capitalism is the unequal sharing of blessings; the inherent vice of socialism is the equal sharing of miseries. SIR WINSTON CHURCHILL

Capitulation: I will be conquered; I will not capitulate. SAMUEL JOHNSON

Career: He knows nothing; and he thinks he knows everything. That points clearly to a political career. GEORGE BERNARD SHAW

Caricature: Caricature is the tribute that mediocrity pays to genius. OSCAR WILDE

Catastrophy: There are few catastrophies so great and irremediable as those that follow an excess of zeal. R. H. BENSON

Cause: It is the cause, not the death that makes the martyr. NAPOLEON BONAPARTE

Celebrity: A celebrity is one who is known to many persons he is glad he doesn't know. H. L. MENCKEN

Celibacy: Marriage has many pains, but celibacy has no pleasures. SAMUEL JOHNSON

Censorship: Art made tongue-tied by authority. WILLIAM SHAKESPEARE

Censorship is like an appendix. When inert, it is useless; when active it is extremely dangerous. MAURICE EDELMAN

They who put out the people's eyes, reproach them of their blindness. JOHN MILTON

Freedom cannot be censored into existence. DWIGHT D. EISENHOWER

Censure: A large part of mankind is angry not with the sins, but with the sinners. SENECA

Censure is the tax a man pays to the public for being eminent. JONATHAN SWIFT

Certainty: If a man will begin with certainties he shall end in doubts; but if he will be content to begin with doubts, he shall end in certainties. FRANCIS BACON

Chance: Chance is a word that does not make sense. Nothing happens without a cause. VOLTAIRE

Chaperone: It's a very venerable and useful superstition that one woman is perfectly safe if another woman is pretending to look after her. HENRY ARTHUR JONES

Character: Every man has three characters: that which he shows, that which he has, and that which he thinks he has. ALPHONSE KARR

Nearly all men can stand adversity, but if you want to test a man's character give him power. ABRAHAM LINCOLN

Charity: Charity is the sterilized milk of human kindness. OLIVER HERFORD

Charity deals with symptoms instead of causes. LORD SAMUEL

Charm: It's a sort of bloom on a woman. If you have it, you don't need to have anything else; and if you don't have it, it doesn't much matter what else you have. SIR J. M. BARRIE

All charming people, I fancy, are spoiled. It is the secret of their attraction. OSCAR WILDE

Chastity: Of all sexual aberrations, perhaps the most peculiar is chastity. REMY DE GOURMONT

Our vocabulary is defective; we give the same name to woman's lack of temptation as to man's lack of opportunity. AMBROSE BIERCE

There are few virtuous women who are not bored with their trade. FRANCOIS

Chatter: They never taste who always drink;
          They always talk who never think. MATTHEW PRIOR

Children: The trouble is, children feel they have to shock their elders, and each generation grows up into something harder to shock. ANON

One way you can often do more for your child is to do less. FRANK CLARK

There are no seven wonders of the world in the eyes of a child. There are seven million. ANON

Little boy to chum: 'The way I see it school is just a mouse race to get us ready for the rat race.'

Children are innocent and love justice, while most adults are wicked and prefer mercy. G. K. CHESTERTON

Don't take up a man's time talking about the smartness of your children; he wants to talk to you about the smartness of his. E. W. HOWE

Children sweeten labours, but they make misfortunes more bitter. FRANCIS BACON

The child has every toy his father wanted. ROBERT E. WHITTEN

What is childhood but a series of happy delusions? SYDNEY SMITH

Before I got married I had six theories about bringing up children; now I have six children, and no theories. EARL OF ROCHESTER

What a melancholy world this would be without children, and what an inhuman world without the aged. SAMUEL TAYLOR COLERIDGE

Bear in mind that children of all ages have one thing in common — they close their ears to advice and open their eyes to example. ANON

Choice: Do not choose to be wrong for the sake of being different. LORD SAMUEL

Christianity: Christianity broke the heart of the world and mended it. G. K. CHESTERTON

Christianity taught men that love is worth more than intelligence. JACQUES MARITAIN

Church: He cannot have God for his father who refuses to have the church for his mother. SAINT AUGUSTINE

While I cannot be regarded as a pillar, I must be regarded as a buttress of the church, because I support it from the outside. LORD MELBOURNE

And of all the plagues with which mankind are cursed,
Ecclesiastic tyranny's the worst. DANIEL DEFOE

A soul cannot be eternally satisfied with kindness, and a soothing murmur, and the singing of hymns. R. H. BENSON

Civil Service: For forms of government let fools contest,
          Whate'er is best administered is best.
          ALEXANDER POPE

Civilization: Civilized we arrived in the Pacific, armed with alcohol, syphilis, trousers and the Bible. HAVELOCK ELLIS

Every new generation is a fresh invasion of savages. HERVEY ALLEN

Increased means and increased leisure are the two civilizers of man. BENJAMIN DISRAELI

Class: For just experience tells, in every soil,
          That those who think must govern those who toil.
          OLIVER GOLDSMITH

There are only two sorts of men: the one the just, who believe themselves sinners; the others sinners, who believe themselves just. BLAISE PASCAL

The world is divided into two classes: those who believe the incredible, and those who do the improbable. OSCAR WILDE

Clergy: The excellency of this text is that it will suit any sermon; and of the sermon, that it will suit any text. LAURENCE STERNE

I have always considered a clergyman as the father of a larger family than he is able to maintain. SAMUEL JOHNSON

Once in seven years I burn all my sermons; for it is a shame if I cannot write better sermons now than I did seven years ago. JOHN WESLEY

Not one clergyman in ten uses his own voice — he uses only an imitation. ELBERT HUBBARD

Clever Dupes: Clever men are the tools with which bad men work. WILLIAM HAZLITT

Climate: I shall continue to praise the English climate till I die, even if I die of the English climate. G. K. CHESTERTON

Comfort: Comfort comes as a guest, lingers to become a host, and stays to enslave us. ANON

Command: It is a fine thing to command, even if it be only a herd of cattle. MIGUEL DE CERVANTES

Commandment: The Eleventh Commandment: Thou shall not be found out. GEORGE WHYTE MELVILLE

Commerce: The selfish spirit of commerce knows no country, and feels no passion or principle but that of gain. THOMAS JEFFERSON

Committee: A committee is a cul de sac to which ideas are lured and then quietly strangled. JOHN A. LINCOLN

Common sense: It is a thousand times better to have common sense without education than to have education without common sense. ROBERT G. INGERSOLL

There is nobody so irritating as somebody with less intelligence and more sense than we have. DON HEROLD

Communication: The big trouble with communication today is the short supply of those willing to be communicated with. DON FRASER

Communism: Russian communism is the illegitimate child of Karl Marx and Catherine the Great. LORD ATTLEE

Communists are people who fancied that they had an unhappy childhood. GERTRUDE STEIN

What is a Communist? One who has yearnings;
For equal division of unequal earnings. EBENEZER ELLIOTT

Competition: There is hardly anything in the world that some man cannot make a little worse and sell a little cheaper. JOHN RUSKIN

Complaining: I was complaining I had no shoes until I met a man who had no feet. ANON

Comprehensive: The old believe everything; the middle-aged suspect everything; the young know everything. OSCAR WILDE

Compromise: A compromise is the art of dividing a cake in such a way that everyone believes that he has got the biggest share. ANON

All government – indeed, every human benefit and enjoyment, every virtue and every prudent act – is founded on compromise and barter. EDMUND BURKE

Conference: A conference is a gathering of important people who singly can do nothing, but together can decide that nothing can be done. FRED ALLEN

Take counsel in wine, but resolve afterwards in water. BENJAMIN FRANKLIN

Confession: A husband should tell his wife everything that he is sure she will find out, and before anyone else does. LORD DEWAR

It is the confession, not the priest, that gives us absolution. OSCAR WILDE

We only confess our little faults to persuade people that we have no big ones. FRANCOIS

Confidant: Most people enjoy the inferiority of their best friends. LORD CHESTERFIELD

As soon as you can say what you think, and not what some other person has thought for you, you are on the way to being a remarkable man. SIR J. M. BARRIE

About 95 per cent of what's told you in confidence, you couldn't get anyone to listen to anyway. ANON

Conscience: In the courtroom of our conscience, we call only witnesses for the defence. FRANCOIS MAURIAC

Conscience is thoroughly well-bred and soon leaves off talking to those who do not wish to hear it. SAMUEL BUTLER

Conservation: The Nation behaves well if it treats the natural resources as assets which it must turn over to the next generation increased, and not impaired in value. THEODORE ROOSEVELT

Conservatism: Conservative. A statesman who is enamoured of existing evils, as distinguished from a Liberal, who wishes to replace them with others. AMBROSE BIERCE

Some fellows get credit for being conservative when they are only stupid. F. McKINNEY HUBBARD

Sir, we must beware of needless innovation, especially when guided by logic. SIR WINSTON CHURCHILL

What is Conservatism? Is it not adherence to the old and tried, against the new and untried? ABRAHAM LINCOLN

Constraint: Necessity is the plea for every infringement of human freedom. It is the argument of tyrants; it is the creed of slaves. WILLIAM PITT

Contentment: Contentment is the true philosopher's stone. The poor are rich that have it, and the rich are poor without it. ANON

Contract: The older you are the more slowly you read a contract. ANON

Contradiction: One often contradicts an opinion when what is uncongenial is really the tone in which it was conveyed. FRIEDRICH NIETZSCHE

Control: When angry count four; when very angry, swear. MARK TWAIN

Conversation: Conversation is a form of communication in which some men never stop to think and many women never think to stop. ANON

No man would listen to you talk if he didn't know it was his turn next. E. W. HOWE

Your ignorance cramps my conversation. SIR ANTHONY HOPE HAWKINS

Conviction: The people who are most bigoted are those who have no conviction at all. G. K. CHESTERTON

Rich men without convictions are more dangerous in modern society than poor women without chastity. GEORGE BERNARD SHAW

Corruption: Bad officials are ones elected by good citizens who do not vote. GEORGE JEAN NATHAN

Country: I should like my country well enough if it were not for my countrymen. HORACE WALPOLE

Courage: Courage is almost a contradiction in terms. It means a strong desire to live taking the form of readiness to die. G. K. CHESTERTON

Perfect courage is to do without witnesses what one would be capable of doing with the world looking on. FRANCOIS

Courage is what it takes to stand up and speak; courage is what it also takes to sit down and listen. ANON

Unfortunately courage is all too often composed of equal parts of whisky and water. ANON

Courage of Conviction: Fortunately for themselves and the world, nearly all men are cowards and dare not act on what they believe. Nearly all our disasters come of a few fools having the 'courage of their convictions'. COVENTRY PATMORE

Courtship: A period during which a girl decides whether she can do better or not. ANON

Crank: The man with a new idea is a crank until the idea succeeds. MARK TWAIN

Creation: The creation of a thousand forests is in one acorn. RALPH WALDO EMERSON

Credibility: It is hard to believe that a man is telling the truth when you know that you would lie if you were in his place. H. L. MENCKEN

Credit: A person who can't pay gets another person who can't pay to guarantee that he can pay. CHARLES DICKENS

Creditors: Definition of a preferential creditor: the first person to be told there's no money left. ANON

Creditors have better memories than debtors. BENJAMIN FRANKLIN

Credulity: The most positive men are the most credulous. ALEXANDER POPE

I have known a vast quantity of nonsense talked about bad men not looking you in the face. Don't trust that conventional idea. Dishonesty will stare honesty out of countenance any day in the week if there is anything to be got by it. CHARLES DICKENS

Cricket: Cricket is a game which the British, not being a spiritual people, had to invent in order to have some concept of eternity. LORD MANCROFT

Criticism: He has a right to criticize who has a heart to help. BENJAMIN FRANKLIN

Criticism may not be agreeable, but it is necessary. It fulfills the same function as pain in the human body; it calls attention to an unhealthy state of things. SIR WINSTON CHURCHILL

Critics: A man must serve his time to every trade
Save censure − critics all are ready made. LORD BYRON

Curiosity: Curiosity is one of the most permanent and certain characteristics of a vigorous intellect. ANON

Cynic: A cynic is just a man who found out when he was about ten that there wasn't any Santa Claus, and he's still upset. JAMES GOULD COZZENS

Cynicism: If a man can see both sides of a problem, you know that none of his money is tied up in it. VERDA ROSS

If there is 'always room at the top', why is there so much shoving going on there? ANON

If you have someone eating out of your hands, it's a good idea to count your fingers. ANON

There's no hiding place in better use than small print. ANON

Just pretending to be rich keeps some people poor. ANON

When I was a boy I was told that anybody could become President; I'm beginning to believe it. CLARENCE DARROW

Dead: One owes respect to the living; but to the dead one owes nothing but the truth. VOLTAIRE

Death: Teach me to live that I may dread
　　　The grave as little as my bed. BISHOP THOMAS KEN

Death never takes the wise man by surprise; he is always ready to go. JEAN DE LA FONTAINE

Death is the veil which those who live call life;
They sleep, and it is lifted. P. B. SHELLEY

Debts: Some people use half their ingenuity to get into debt, and the other half to avoid paying it. GEORGE D. PRENTICE

A creditor is worse than a slave-owner; for the master owns only your person, but a creditor owns your dignity, and can command it. VICTOR HUGO

Speak not of my debts unless you mean to pay them. ENGLISH PROVERB

Deceive: If a man deceives me once shame on him; if he deceives me twice, shame on me. ITALIAN PROVERB

Decent: One shouldn't be too inquisitive in life,
　　　Either about God's secrets or one's wife.
　　　GEOFFREY CHAUCER

A truth that's told with bad intent,
Beats all the lies you can invent. WILLIAM BLAKE

Deeds: The smallest deed is better than the grandest intention.
ANON

Begin not with a programme, but with a deed. FLORENCE NIGHTINGALE

What this troubled old world needs,
is less of quibbling over creeds;
Fewer words and better deeds. KEBLE

Defamation: Lie lustily, some filth will stick. THOMAS HALL

Defeat: What reinforcement we may gain from hope;
　　　If not, what resolution from despair. JOHN MILTON

Deliberation: Deliberation. The act of examining one's bread to determine which side it is buttered on. AMBROSE BIERCE

Democracy: Speakers Corner: The adventure playground of democracy. JOHN CUNNINGHAM

Man's capacity for evil makes democracy necessary; man's capacity for good makes democracy possible. DR RHEINHOLD NIEBUR

Democracy is the recurrent suspicion that more than half of the people are right more than half of the time. E. B. WHITE

Democracy is the power of equal votes for unequal minds. ANON

Democracy is only an experiment in government, and it has the obvious disadvantage of merely counting votes instead of weighing them. DEAN W. R. INGE

Democracy: in which you say what you like and do what you're told. SIR GERALD BARRY

Democracy substitutes election by the incompetent many for appointment by the corrupt few. GEORGE BERNARD SHAW

No man is good enough to govern another man without the other's consent. ABRAHAM LINCOLN

Two cheers for democracy: one because it admits variety and two because it permits criticism. E. M. FORSTER

Democracy means simply the bludgeoning of the people by the people for the people. OSCAR WILDE

Let the people think they govern and they will be governed. WILLIAM PENN

Democracy becomes a government of bullies tempered by editors. RALPH WALDO EMERSON

Detection: When you have eliminated the impossible, whatever remains, however improbable, must be the truth. SIR ARTHUR CONAN DOYLE

Devil: Most people sell their souls, and live with a good conscience on the proceeds. LOGAN PEARSALL SMITH

Diagnosis: A physician's forecast of disease by the patient's pulse and purse. AMBROSE BIERCE

Those in possession of absolute power can not only prophesy and make their prophesies come true, but they can also lie and make their lies come true. ERIC HOFFER

Difficult: Not everything that is more difficult is more meritorious. SAINT THOMAS AQUINAS

Difficulties: As a final incentive before giving up a difficult task, try to imagine it successfully accomplished by someone you violently dislike. K. ZENIOS

Dinner: It isn't so much what's on the table that matters as what's on the chairs. SIR W. S. GILBERT

A man seldom thinks with more earnestness of anything than he does of his dinner. SAMUEL JOHNSON

Diplomat: A diplomat is a man who always remembers a woman's birthday but never remembers her age. ROBERT FROST

A really good diplomat does not go in for victories, even when he wins them. WALTER LIPPMAN

A diplomat these days is nothing but a head-waiter who's allowed to sit down occasionally. PETER USTINOV

Director: I always suspect a director who says he can afford to be away from the office only for a week at a time. This generally means either that he is a frightened man or else he is thoroughly inefficient and incapable of delegation. SIR RICHARD POWELL

I have found some of the best reasons I ever had for remaining at the bottom simply by looking at the men at the top. FRANK MOORE COLBY

Discipline: He that complies against his will,
Is of his own opinion still. SAMUEL BUTLER

Disclaimer: When a fellow says, 'It ain't the money but the principle of the thing', it's the money. F. McKINNEY HUBBARD

Discretion: What is called discretion in men is called cunning in animals. JEAN DE LA FONTAINE

A wise man sees as much as he ought, not as much as he can. MICHEL DE MONTAIGNE

Be wiser than other people, if you can, but do not tell them so. LORD CHESTERFIELD

Disgust: No man hates God without first hating himself. BISHOP FULTON SHEEN

Diversion: He that cries out 'stop thief', is often he that has stolen the treasure. WILLIAM CONGREVE

Doctor: The doctor found when she was dead, her last disorder mortal. OLIVER GOLDSMITH

Either he's dead or my watch has stopped. GROUCHO MARX

If prolonged it cannot be severe, and if severe, it cannot be prolonged. SENECA

The art of medicine consists of amusing the patient while Nature cures the disease. VOLTAIRE

While the doctors consult, the patient dies. ENGLISH PROVERB

He's a fool that makes his doctor his heir. BENJAMIN FRANKLIN

No doctor is a good doctor who has never been ill himself. CONFUCIUS

Doctors think a lot of patients are cured who have simply quit in disgust. DON HEROLD

Dog: If you pick up a starving dog and make him prosperous, he will not bite you; that is the principal difference between a dog and a man. MARK TWAIN

Dogma: Dogma does not mean the absence of thought, but the end of thought. G. K. CHESTERTON

Drama: Drama is life with the dull bits cut out. ALFRED HITCHCOCK

Dreams: Dreaming permits each and every one of us to be safely insane every night of the week. ANON

Dress: She looked as though she had been poured into her clothes and had forgotten to say 'when'. P. G. WODEHOUSE

Drink: An honest man, that is not quite sober, has nothing to fear. JOSEPH ADDISON

Drinking: There are two reasons for drinking: one is when you are thirsty, to cure it; the other, when you are not thirsty, to prevent it . . . prevention is better than cure. THOMAS LOVE PEACOCK

Drunkenness: Drunkenness is nothing but voluntary madness. SENECA

Dullness: There are no uninteresting things, there are only uninterested people. G. K. CHESTERTON

Dumb: The next time you call your dog a dumb animal, remember who he's got working to support him. ANON

Dunce: How much a dunce that has been set to roam excels a dunce that has been kept at home. WILLIAM COWPER

Duty: Duty. That which sternly impels us in the direction of profit, along the line of desire. AMBROSE BIERCE

Economics: There's one way to solve all the economic problems of the country. Make complacency taxable. ANON

Economics is the art of satisfying infinite wants with limited resources. ANON

Economy: There is no profit in going to bed early to save candles if the result is twins. ANON

Education: The secret of education lies in respecting the pupil. If a man's education is finished, he is finished. E. A. FILENE

The first thing education teaches you to do is walk alone. ALFRED ALOYSIUS HERN

We educate one another; and we cannot do this if half of us consider the other half not good enough to talk to. GEORGE BERNARD SHAW

Educate men without religion and you make them clever devils. DUKE OF WELLINGTON

Human history becomes more and more a race between education and catastrophe. H. G. WELLS

Education makes a people easy to lead, but difficult to drive; easy to govern but impossible to enslave. LORD BROUGHAM

It is not the insurrections of ignorance that are dangerous, but the revolts of intelligence. J. R. LOWELL

British parents are very ready to call for a system of education which offers equal opportunity to all children but their own. LORD ECCLES

Egotist: An egotist is a man who thinks as much of himself as you think of yourself. ANON

A person of low taste, more interested in himself than me. AMBROSE BIERCE

I have nothing to declare except my genius. OSCAR WILDE

Election promises: Vote for the man who promises least, he'll be the least disappointing. BERNARD BARUCH

Electorate: Where there is no vision, the people perish. THE BIBLE—PROVERBS

Eloquence: Can there be a more horrible object in existence than an eloquent man not speaking the truth? THOMAS CARLYLE

The finest eloquence is that which gets things done; the worst is that which delays them. DAVID LLOYD GEORGE

When a man gets talking about himself, he seldom fails to be eloquent and often reaches the sublime. JOSH BILLINGS

Embarrassment: The finest fruit of serious learning should be the ability to speak the word 'God' without reserve or embarrassment. ANON

Emotion: The young man who has not wept is a savage, and the old man who will not laugh is a fool. GEORGE SANTAYANA

Encouragement: Encouragement after censure is like the sun after a shower. ANON

Endurance: We all have enough strength to bear the misfortunes of others. FRANCOIS

Enemy: You must not fight too often with one enemy, or you will teach him all your art of war. NAPOLEON BONAPARTE

You have many enemies, that know not why they are so, but, like to village curs, bark when their fellows do. WILLIAM SHAKESPEARE

England: England surely, is the paradise of little men, and the purgatory of great ones. CARDINAL JOHN NEWMAN

The people of England are never so happy as when you tell them they are ruined. ARTHUR MURPHY

It is to the middle class we must look for the safety of England. W. M. THACKERAY

Of all the nations in the world, at present the English are the stupidist in speech, the wisest in actions. THOMAS CARLYLE

You never find an Englishman among the underdogs − except in England of course. EVELYN WAUGH

Not only England, but every Englishman is an island. FRIEDRICH VON HARDENBERG

To be an Englishman is to belong to the most exclusive club there is. OGDEN NASH

England at war: We do not covet anything from any nation except their respect. SIR WINSTON CHURCHILL

Enterprise: There are two kinds of men who never amount to much: those who cannot do what they are told, and those who can do nothing else. CYRUS H. CURTIS

Entertain: To entertain some people, all you have to do is listen. ANON

Enthusiasts: Enthusiasts without capacity are the really dangerous people. ANON

It is unfortunate, considering that enthusiasm moves the world, that so few enthusiasts can be trusted to speak the truth. A. J. BALFOUR

Epigram: True wit is nature to advantage dressed,
　　　　What oft was thought but ne'er so well expressed.
　　　ALEXANDER POPE

Epitaph: Here lies the body of Samuel Jay,
　　　　Who died maintaining his right of way.

Equality: Women's 'Lib' claims equal rights; so why are diamonds a girl's best friend – but a man's best friend is a dog? ANON

All men are born equal but the tough job is to outgrow it. DON LEARY

Error: A man should never be ashamed to own he has been in the wrong, which is but saying, in other words, that he is wiser today than he was yesterday. JONATHAN SWIFT

The first faults are theirs that commit them, the second theirs that permit them. ENGLISH PROVERB

Establishment: There's nothing like becoming established to cure one's dissatisfaction with the establishment. HAROLD COFFIN

All establishments die of dignity. They are too proud to think themselves ill, and to take a little physic. SYDNEY SMITH

Estate: If a man owns land, the land owns him. RALPH WALDO EMERSON

Estrangement: Loneliness is to endure the presence of one who does not understand. ELBERT HUBBARD

Evasion: A grocer was asked why his prices were always higher at week-ends. He replied, 'They aren't higher at week-ends, they're lower during the week.'

Evidence: I will look at any additional evidence to confirm the opinion to which I have already come. LORD MOLSON when a junior minister

Evil: There are a thousand hacking at the branches of evil to one who is striking at the root. ANON

Examination: Examinations are formidable even to the best prepared, for the greatest fool may ask more than the wisest man can answer. C. C. COLTON

Many of us look at the Ten Commandments as an exam paper; eight only to be attempted. MALCOLM MUGGERIDGE

Example: Few things are harder to put up with than the annoyance of a good example. MARK TWAIN

Example is not the main thing in influencing others, it's the only thing. ALBERT SCHWEITZER

'For example' is not proof. JEWISH PROVERB

An old man gives good advice to console himself for no longer being able to set a good example. FRANCOIS

Excuse: There is hardly any man so strict as not to vary a little from truth when he is to make an excuse. LORD HALIFAX

Executive: A molehill man is a pseudo-busy executive who comes to work at 9am and finds a molehill on his desk. He has until 5pm to make this molehill into a mountain. An accomplished molehill man will often have his mountain finished before lunch. FRED ALLEN

Executive ability is deciding quickly and getting somebody else to do the work. J. G. POLLOCK

Exercise: Running after women never hurt anybody – it's catching 'em that does the damage. JACK DAVIES

Experience: See and do all you can; never miss a new experience. That is education, and something no one can rob you of however poor you might become. ANON

I had rather have a fool to make me merry than experience to make me sad. WILLIAM SHAKESPEARE

Experience is the name everyone gives to their mistakes. OSCAR WILDE

Experience. The wisdom that enables us to recognize in an undesirable old aquaintance the folly that we have already embraced. AMBROSE BIERCE

It is costly wisdom that is bought by experience. ROGER ASCHAM

Experience comprises illusions lost, rather than wisdom gained. JOSEPH ROUSE

Experience is a comb which nature gives to men when they are bald. EASTERN PROVERB

Experiment: The best way to convince a fool that he is wrong is to let him have his own way. JOSH BILLINGS

Extravagance: An extravagance is anything you buy that is of no earthly use to your wife. FRANKLIN P. JONES

My main problem is reconciling my gross habits with my net income. ERROL FLYNN

Extremism: Extremism in the defense of liberty is no vice. Moderation in the pursuit of justice is no virtue. SENATOR BARRY GOLDWATER

Face: I have always considered my face a convenience rather than an ornament. DR OLIVER WENDELL HOLMES

Fact: Maternity is a matter of fact; paternity a matter of opinion. ANON

No wife can endure a gambling husband unless he is a steady winner. LORD DEWAR

Failure: Overheard: 'He isn't a failure. He just started at the bottom and liked it there.'

He was a self-made man who owed his lack of success to nobody. JOSEPH HELLER

Faith: Faith. Belief without evidence in what is told by one who speaks without knowledge, of things without parallel. AMBROSE BIERCE

Faith is the substance of things hoped for, the evidence of things not seen. THE BIBLE—HEBREWS

To believe only possibilities is not Faith, but mere philosophy. SIR THOMAS BROWNE

Faith begins as an experiment and ends as an experience. DEAN W. R. INGE

Faith may be defined briefly as an illogical belief in the occurrence of the improbable. H. L. MENCKEN

Faith is often the boast of the man who is too lazy to investigate. F. M. KNOWLES

The faith that stands on authority is not faith. RALPH WALDO EMERSON

Fame: Fame is proof that the people are gullible. RALPH WALDO EMERSON

The great are only great because we carry them on our shoulders. CLAUDE DUBOSCO-MONTANDRA

Fanatic: Fanatics are men with strong tastes for drink trying hard to keep sober. ELBERT HUBBARD

A fanatic is a man that does what he thinks the Lord would do if he knew the facts of the case. FINLEY PETER DUNNE

A fanatic is one who can't change his mind and won't change the subject. SIR WINSTON CHURCHILL

Defined in psychological terms, a fanatic is a man who consciously over-compensates a secret doubt. ALDOUS HUXLEY

Fanaticism: Fanaticism consists in redoubling your effort when you have forgotten your aim. GEORGE SANTAYANA

Farewell: It is amazing how nice people are to you when they know you are going away. MICHAEL ARLEN

If you'd lose a troublesome visitor, lend him money. BENJAMIN FRANKLIN

Fascism: Fascism is not in itself a new order of society. It is the future refusing to be born. ANEURIN BEVAN

Fashion: Fashion is gentility running away from vulgarity, and afraid of being overtaken. WILLIAM HAZLITT

Fashion is that by which the fantastic becomes for a moment the universal. OSCAR WILDE

A fashion is nothing but an induced epidemic. GEORGE BERNARD SHAW

Father: We think our fathers fools, so wise we grow;
　　　　Our wiser sons, no doubt will think us so.
　　　ALEXANDER POPE

In peace the sons bury their fathers, but in war the fathers bury their sons. CROESUS 560BC

What harsh judges fathers are to all young men. TERENCE 185–159BC

The fundamental defect of fathers is that they want their children to be a credit to them. BERTRAND RUSSELL

No man is responsible for his father. That is entirely his mother's affair. MARGARET TURNBULL

Faults: The greatest of faults is to be conscious of none. THOMAS CARLYLE

Almost all our faults are more pardonable than the methods we think up to hide them. ANON

Men do not suspect faults which they do not commit. SAMUEL JOHNSON

Fear: Those who love to be feared, fear to be loved. Some fear them, but they fear everyone. JEAN PIERRE CAMUS

We fear that which we do not understand. ANON

Nothing in life is to be feared. It is only to be understood. ANON

To know what is right and not to do it is the worst cowardice. ANON

Feelings: Half our mistakes in life arise from feeling where we ought to think, and thinking where we ought to feel. J. CHURTON COLLINS

Femininity: You sometimes have to answer a woman according to her womanishness, just as you have to answer a fool according to his folly. GEORGE BERNARD SHAW

There are only three things in the world that women do not understand, and they are Liberty, Equality, and Fraternity. G. K. CHESTERTON

Fidelity: Fidelity. A virtue peculiar to those who are about to be betrayed. AMBROSE BIERCE

Flattery: He who knows how to flatter also knows how to slander. NAPOLEON BONAPARTE

Fool: No woman can turn a fool into a wise man, but any woman can turn a wise man into a fool. ANON

However big the fool, there is always a bigger fool to admire him. NICOLAS BOILEAU

A learned fool is one who has read everything, and simply remembered it. JOSH BILLINGS

There are two kinds of fool: one says, 'This is old, therefore it is good'; the other says, 'This is new, therefore it is better.' DEAN W. R. INGE

There are more fools than knaves in the world, else the knaves would not have enough to live on. SAMUEL BUTLER

Force: Who overcomes by force hath overcome but half his foe. ANON

Foreigners: Modern man . . . is educated to understand foreign languages and misunderstand foreigners. G. K. CHESTERTON

The farther I journey towards the West, the more convinced I am that the 'wise men' came from the East. WILLIAM DAVY, sergeant-at-law

Forgetfulness: Life cannot go on without a great deal of forgetting. HONORÉ DE BALZAC

Forgetfulness. A gift of God bestowed upon debtors in compensation for their destitution of conscience. AMBROSE BIERCE

Forgiveness: Always forgive your enemies; nothing annoys them so much. ANON

How shall I lose the sin, yet keep the sense,
And love the offender, yet detest the offence? ALEXANDER POPE

It is very easy to forgive others their mistakes: it takes more grit and gumption to forgive them for having witnessed your own. ANON

To err is human; to forgive divine. ALEXANDER POPE

Fortune: An aim in life is the only fortune worth finding. ROBERT LOUIS STEVENSON

Frankness: We appreciate frankness from those who like us, frankness from others is called insolence. ANON

Freedom: Freedom is not worth having if it does not connote freedom to err. MAHATMA GANDHI

The basic test of freedom is perhaps less in what we are free to do than in what we are free not to do. ERIC HOFFER

Give me the liberty to know, to utter, and to argue according to conscience, above all liberties. JOHN MILTON

Friendless: Friendless. Having no favors to bestow. Destitute of fortune. Addicted to utterance of truth and common sense. AMBROSE BIERCE

Friendship: Thy friendship oft has made my heart to ache:
Do be my enemy – for friendship's sake.
WILLIAM BLAKE

It is well, when one is judging a friend, to remember that he is judging you with the same godlike and superior impartiality. ARNOLD BENNETT

If you would have friends, first learn to do without them. ELBERT HUBBARD

A friend that ain't in need is a friend indeed. F. McKINNEY HUBBARD

God defend me from my friends; from my enemies I can defend myself. SIXTEENTH-CENTURY PROVERB

In prosperity our friends know us; in adversity we know our friends. J. CHURTON COLLINS

Instead of loving your enemies, treat your friends a little better. E. W. HOWE

A friend is a person with whom I may be sincere. Before him I may think aloud. RALPH WALDO EMERSON

A man's friend likes him but leaves him as he is: his wife loves him and is always trying to turn him into somebody else. G. K. CHESTERTON

Nothing is more dangerous than a friend without discretion; even a prudent enemy is preferable. JEAN DE LA FONTAINE

The finest kind of friendship is between people who expect a great deal from each other but never ask it. ANON

The proper office of a friend is to side with you when you are in the wrong. Nearly anybody will side with you when you are right. ANON

True friendship comes when silence between two people is comfortable. ANON

Friendships multiply joys and divide griefs. H. C. BOHN

The path of social advancement is, and must be, strewn with broken friendships. H. G. WELLS

Functions: Public life is the paradise of voluble windbags. GEORGE BERNARD SHAW

If you're there before it's over, you're on time. MAYOR JIMMY J. WALKER

Funerals: Funeral pomp is more for the vanity of the living than for the honour of the dead. LA ROCHEFOUCAULD

Future: It is always wise to look ahead, but difficult to look further than you can see. SIR WINSTON CHURCHILL

What you give to the future is but the debt you owe to the past. ANON

That period of time in which our affairs prosper, our friends are true and our happiness is assured. AMBROSE BIERCE

Gardening: One of the healthiest ways to gamble is with a spade and a packet of garden seeds. DAN BEUNETT

Gardens: Love of flowers and vegetables is not enough to make a good gardener. He must also hate weeds. EUGENE P. BERTIN

Genius: To do what others cannot do is talent, to do what talent cannot do is genius. WILL HENRY

Genius does what it must, and talent what it can. ANON

Gentlemen: Education begins a gentleman, conversation completes him. ENGLISH PROVERB

A gentleman is one who never hurts anyone's feelings unintentionally. OSCAR WILDE

I can make a lord, but only God Almighty can make a gentleman. KING JAMES I OF ENGLAND

The only infallible rule we know is, that the man who is always talking about being a gentleman never is one. R. S. SURTEES

Girls: Secrets with girls, like loaded guns with boys, are never valued till they make a noise. GEORGE CRABBE

Giving: One must be poor to know the luxury of giving. ANON

God: O God, for as much as without Thee,
      We are not enabled to doubt Thee,
      Help us all by Thy grace,
      To convince the whole race,
      It knows nothing whatever about Thee.
      FATHER RONALD KNOX

I have never understood why it should be considered derogatory to the Creator to suppose that he has a sense of humour.
DEAN W. R. INGE

Women give themselves to God when the devil wants nothing more to do with them. SOPHIE ARNOULD

There is nothing so small but that we can honour God by asking His guidance of it, or insult Him by taking it into our own hands.
JOHN RUSKIN

And almost every one when age, disease, or sorrows strike him; inclines to think there is a God, or something very like Him.
A. H. CLOUGH

And lips say 'God be pitiful,'
Who ne'er said 'God be praised.' ELIZABETH BARRETT BROWNING

Golf: From a British Golf Club bulletin: 'As in previous years, the evening concluded with a toast to the new President in champagne provided by the retiring President, drunk as usual before midnight.'

A day spent in a round of strenuous idleness. WILLIAM WORDSWORTH

Golf is a good walk spoiled. MARK TWAIN

Good: To be good only to yourself is to be good for nothing.
VOLTAIRE

Good taste: A man of great common-sense and good taste – meaning thereby a man without originality or moral courage.
GEORGE BERNARD SHAW

Goodwill: Moral of the work. In war: resolution. In defeat:

defiance. In victory: magnanimity. In peace: goodwill. SIR WINSTON CHURCHILL

Gossip: In scandal as in robbery, the receiver is always thought as bad as the thief. LORD CHESTERFIELD

Gossip is that which no one claims to like – but everybody enjoys. ANON

Government: The object of government in peace and in war is not the glory of rulers or of races, but the happiness of the common man. SIR WILLIAM BEVERIDGE

The authorities were at their wit's end, nor had it taken them long to get there. DESMOND McCARTHY

If you would rule the world quietly, you must keep it amused. RALPH WALDO EMERSON

Men are not governed by justice, but by law or persuasion. When they refuse to be governed by law or persuasion, they have to be governed by force or fraud, or both. GEORGE BERNARD SHAW

The three ends which a statesman ought to propose to himself in the government of a Nation are security to possessors, facility to acquirers, and hope to all. SAMUEL TAYLOR COLERIDGE

At the very heart of British Government there is a luxuriant and voluntary exclusion of talent. PROFESSOR BRIAN CHAPMAN

Whenever people are well informed they can be trusted with their own government. THOMAS JEFFERSON

Gratitude: Too great a hurry to discharge an obligation is a kind of ingratitude. FRANCOIS

We seldom find people ungrateful so long as we are in a condition to render them service. LA ROCHEFOUCAULD

In most of mankind gratitude is merely a secret hope of further favours. FRANCOIS

Greatness: The greatness of a man can nearly always be measured by his willingness to be kind. ANON

There is a great man who makes every man feel small. But the really great man is the man who makes every man feel great. CHARLES DICKENS

I cannot hear what you say for the thunder of what you are. ZULU PROVERB

There is no greatness where simplicity, goodness and truth are absent. LEO TOLSTOY

Grief: Nothing becomes so offensive so quickly as grief. When fresh it finds some one to console it, but when it becomes chronic, it is ridiculed, and rightly. SENECA

The display of grief makes more demands than grief itself. How few men are sad in their own company. SENECA

Grief is the agony of an instant; the indulgence of grief the blunder of a life. BENJAMIN DISRAELI

Groom's response: What we have done this afternoon is to renounce happiness, renounce freedom, renounce tranquility, above all renounce the romantic possibilities of an unknown future, for the cares of a household and a family. I beg that no man may sieze the occasion to get half drunk and utter imbecile speeches and coarse pleasantries at my expense. GEORGE BERNARD SHAW

Guilt: Guilt has very quick ears to an accusation. HENRY FIELDING

Habit: The chains of habit are too weak to be felt until they are too strong to be broken. SAMUEL JOHNSON

Nothing so needs reforming as other people's habits. MARK TWAIN

Happiness: True happiness consists in something to do, something to love, and something to hope for. ANON

Happiness is a mystery, like religion, and should never be rationalized. G. K. CHESTERTON

The secret of being miserable is to have leisure to bother about whether you are happy or not. The cure for it is occupation. GEORGE BERNARD SHAW

Happiness has a habit of pursuing the person who feels grateful to his God, comfortable with his conscience, in favour with his friends, in love with his labours, and in balance with his bank. ANON

Learn to be happy alone. If we do not enjoy our own company, why inflict it on others? ANON

He who seeks only for applause from without has all his happiness in another's keeping. OLIVER GOLDSMITH

The greatest happiness of the greatest number is the foundation of morals and legislation. JEREMY BENTHAM

Hard work: The power to work hard may not be talent, but it is the best possible substitute for it. ANON

Hatred: Now hatred is by far the longest pleasure;
      Men love in haste, but they detest at leisure.
      LORD BYRON

Health: Attention to health is the greatest hindrance to life. PLATO

Heart: The heart has its reasons which reason does not know. BLAISE PASCAL

Heaven: Heaven is the place where the donkey at last catches up with the carrot. ANON

Hell: A fool's paradise is a wise man's hell. THOMAS FULLER

Help: The hands that help are holier than the lips that pray. R. G. INGERSOLL

Help a man against his will and you do the same as murder him. HORACE

Historian: History repeats itself; historians repeat each other. PHILIP GUEDALLA

A historian is a prophet in reverse. FRIEDRICH VON SCHLEGEL

History: The essential matter of history is not what happened but what people thought or said about it. FREDERIC W. MAITLAND

All history is a record of the power of minorities, and of minorities of one. RALPH WALDO EMERSON

History which is, indeed, little more than the register of the crimes, follies, and misfortunes of mankind. EDWARD GIBBON

If a man could say nothing against a character but what he can prove, history could not be written. SAMUEL JOHNSON

The principal office of history I take to be this: to prevent virtuous actions from being forgotten, and that evil words and deeds should fear an infamous reputation with posterity. TACITUS

Home: Home is not where you live, but where they understand you. ANON

Hope: Hope springs eternal in the human breast;
      Man never is, but always to be blest. ALEXANDER POPE

Hospitality: Hospitality consists in a little fire, a little food, and an immense quiet. RALPH WALDO EMERSON

Humanity: Mankind will not be reasoned out of the feelings of humanity. SIR WILLIAM BLACKSTONE

Humility: Humility must always be the portion of any man who receives acclaim earned in the blood of his followers and the sacrifices of his friends. DWIGHT D. EISENHOWER

Humility has depressed many a genius to a hermit, but never raised one to fame. WILLIAM SHENSTONE

Humour: Humour is an affirmation of dignity, a declaration of a man's superiority to all that befalls him. ANON

Humour cannot be learnt. Besides wit and keenness of mind, it pre-supposes a large measure of goodness of heart, of patience, of tolerance and human kindness. ANON

Husband: Being a husband is a whole-time job. That is why so many husbands fail. They cannot give their entire attention to it. ARNOLD BENNETT

A husband is what is left of the lover after the nerve has been extracted. HELEN ROWLAND

The only solid and lasting peace between a man and his wife is doubtless a separation. LORD CHESTERFIELD

I began as a passion and ended as a habit, like all husbands. GEORGE BERNARD SHAW

The calmest husbands make the stormiest wives. PROVERB

Hypocrisy: Hypocrisy is a homage that vice pays to virtue. PROVERB

Idealist: An idealist is a person who helps other people to be prosperous. HENRY FORD

Ideas: It is with ideas, as with umbrellas; if left lying about they are peculiarly liable to a change of ownership. ANON

Idleness: To be idle and to be poor have always been reproaches, and therefore every man endeavours with his utmost care to hide his poverty from others, and his idleness from himself. SAMUEL JOHNSON

Ignorance: Ignorance is bold, and knowledge reserved. ANON

Everybody is ignorant, only on different subjects. ANON

Great minds are oppressed by their ignorance, small minds by their knowledge. ANON

Imitation: To be exactly the opposite is also a form of imitation. GEORGE LICHTENBURG

Immortality: The average man, who does not know what to do with this life, wants another one which shall last forever. ANATOLE FRANCE

Either the soul is immortal and we shall not die, or it perishes with the flesh, and we shall not know then that we are dead. Live then, as if you were eternal. ANDRE MAUROIS

Impossible: There is a vulgar incredulity, which in historical matters, as well as those of religion, finds it easier to doubt than to examine. SIR WALTER SCOTT

Impression: You never get a second chance to make a good first impression. ANON

Overheard at a party: 'The reason I'll never be rich is that my wife thinks we have to create the impression that we already are.'

Incentive: By working faithfully eight hours a day, you may eventually get to be a boss and work twelve hours a day. ROBERT FROST

Incompatibility: Incompatibility. In matrimony a similarity of tastes, particularly the taste for domination. AMBROSE BIERCE

Indifference: The worst sin towards our fellow creatures is not to hate them, but to be indifferent to them; that's the essence of inhumanity. GEORGE BERNARD SHAW

Inexperience: The young are always ready to give those who are older the full benefit of their inexperience. OSCAR WILDE

Inexplicable: It is beyond our power to explain either the prosperity of the wicked or the afflictions of the righteous. TALMUD

Inflation: Inflation is caused by people who believe in the romantic theory that some day wages will catch up with prices. ANON

Surely inflation must be the world's most successful thief. CARL PERSON

Injury: He threatens many that hath injured one. BEN JONSON

Injustice: I know no method to secure the repeal of bad or obnoxious laws so effective as their stringent execution. ULYSSES S. GRANT

Innocence: It makes a great difference whether a person is unwilling to sin, or does not know how. SENECA

He could be a pianist in a brothel without knowing what goes on upstairs. ANON

Insanity: Insanity is often the logic of an accurate mind overtaxed. DR OLIVER WENDELL HOLMES

It is his reasonable conversation which mostly frightens us in a madman. ANATOLE FRANCE

Inspiration: The inspirations of today are the shams of tomorrow – the purpose has departed. ELBERT HUBBARD

Instinct: Instinct is the nose of the mind. ANON

The natural man has only two primal passions – to get and to beget. SIR WILLIAM OSLER

Insults: Never insult an alligator until after you have crossed the river. CORDELL HULL

Integrity: A task becomes a duty from the moment you suspect it to be an essential part of that integrity which alone entitles a man to assume responsibility. ANON

Investment: Money is like muck, not much good except it be spread. FRANCIS BACON

Invincibility: History shows that there are no invincible armies. JOSEPH STALIN

Irish: The Irish are a fair people; they never speak well of one another. SAMUEL JOHNSON

Jews: The Jews generally give value. They make you pay; but they deliver the goods. In my experience the men who want something for nothing are invariably Christians. GEORGE BERNARD SHAW

Jockeys: All the best 'jockeys' are on the ground giving advice to those mounted. ANON

Journalism: Headlines twice the size of the events. JOHN GALSWORTHY

There is but one way for a newspaper man to look at a politician, and that is down. FRANK H. SIMONDS

You cannot hope to bribe or twist (thank God) the British journalist. But seeing what the man will do unbribed, there's no occasion to. HUMBERT WOLFE

Judge: A Judge is not supposed to know anything about the facts of life until they have been presented in evidence and explained to him at least three times. LORD CHIEF JUSTICE PARKER

Judgement: We judge ourselves by what we feel capable of doing, while others judge us by what we have done. LONGFELLOW

Don't judge everything by appearances, the early bird may simply have been up all night. ANON

Judgement comes from experience. Experience comes from poor judgement. ANON

The truest test of independent judgement is being able to dislike someone who admires us, and admire someone who dislikes us. ANON

At twenty years of age, the will reigns; at thirty the wit; and at forty, the judgement. HENRY GRATTAN

Jury: The public do not know enough to be experts, yet know enough to decide between them. SAMUEL BUTLER

A jury consists of twelve persons chosen to decide who has the better lawyer. ROBERT FROST

Justice: Justice is truth in action. ANON

Justice is the insurance we have on our lives; and obedience is the premium we pay for it. ANON

Justice is what we get when the decision is in our favour. ANON

The love of justice is, in most men, nothing more than the fear of suffering injustice. FRANCOIS

Justice is my being allowed to do whatever I like. Injustice is whatever prevents my doing so. SAMUEL BUTLER

Justice must tame, whom mercy cannot win. GEORGE SAVILE

Kindness: The greatest pleasure I know is to do a good action by stealth and have it found out by accident. CHARLES LAMB

One of the most difficult things to give away is kindness. It is usually returned. ANON

You can never do a kindness too soon, for you never know how soon it will be too late. RALPH WALDO EMERSON

Kisses: People who throw kisses are hopelessly lazy. BOB HOPE

Knowledge: Knowledge is power, if you know it about the right person. ETHEL WATTS MUMFORD

As knowledge increases, wonder deepens. CHARLES MORGAN

Lady: A lady is a woman who makes a man behave like a gentleman. RUSSELL LYNES

A lady is one who never shows her underwear unintentionally. LILLIAN DAY

Late: He was always late on principle, his principle being that punctuality is the thief of time. OSCAR WILDE

Laughter: Laugh and the world laughs with you;
      Weep and you weep alone;
    For the sad old earth must borrow its mirth,
      But has trouble enough of its own.
ELLA WHEELER WILCOX

Among those whom I like, I can find no common denominator; but among those whom I love, I can. All of them make me laugh. ANON

Laurels: Nothing is harder on your laurels than resting on them. ANON

Law: Law grinds the poor, and rich men rule the law. OLIVER GOLDSMITH

Without law no little souls fresh from God would be branded illegitimate as soon as they reach earth. ELBERT HUBBARD

Laws, like houses, lean on one another. EDMUND BURKE

Lawyer: A lawyer is a learned gentleman who rescues your estate from your enemies and keeps it himself. LORD BROUGHAM

The robes of lawyers are lined with the obstinacy of clients. ENGLISH PROVERB

Lawyers are the only persons in whom ignorance of the law is not punished. JEREMY BENTHAM

A solicitor is a man who calls in a person he doesn't know to sign a contract he hasn't seen to buy property he doesn't want with money he hasn't got. PRESIDENT OF THE LAW SOCIETY

If there were no bad people, there would be no good lawyers. CHARLES DICKENS

Learning: Every day that we spend without learning something is a day lost. BEETHOVEN

What we learn with pleasure we never forget. ALFRED MERCER

Lecturer: A professor is one who talks in someone else's sleep. W. H. AUDEN

Liar: No one lies so boldly as the man who is indignant. FRIEDRICH NIETZSCHE

The woman who cannot evolve a good lie in defence of the man she loves is unworthy of the name of wife. ELBERT HUBBARD

The visionary lies to himself, the liar only to others. FRIEDRICH NIETZSCHE

Libel: Strange that a man who has wit enough to write a satire should have folly enough to publish it. BENJAMIN FRANKLIN

Liberty: A Robin Redbreast in a cage
      Puts all heaven in a rage. WILLIAM BLAKE

Liberty means responsibility. That is why most men dread it. GEORGE BERNARD SHAW

Whenever we take away the liberties of those whom we hate, we are opening the way to loss of liberty for those we love. WENDELL L. WILKIE

LIBERTY

Give me the liberty to know, to utter, to argue freely according to conscience, above all liberties. JOHN MILTON

It is a strange desire to seek power and to lose liberty. FRANCIS BACON

He that would make his own liberty secure, must guard even his enemy from oppression. THOMAS PAINE

Corruption, the most infallible symptom of constitutional liberty. EDWARD GIBBON

Most lies are quite successful, and human society would be impossible without a great deal of good natured lying. GEORGE BERNARD SHAW

By itself, truth always wins; a lie needs an accomplice. ANON

Life: Life demands from you only the strength you possess. Only one feat is possible – not to have to run away. DAG HAMMARSKJOLD

Dost thou love life? Then do not squander Time, for that's the stuff life is made of. BENJAMIN FRANKLIN

The hardest thing to learn in life is which bridge to cross, and which to burn. ANON

Remember, now and always, that life is no idle dream, but a solemn reality, and encompassed by Eternity. Find out your task; stand to it; the night cometh when no man can work. THOMAS CARLYLE

The greatest pleasure of life is to love;
The greatest treasure – contentment;
The greatest possession – health;
The greatest ease – sleep;
The best medicine – a true friend. MICHELMERSH

Life is the art of drawing sufficient conclusions from insufficient premises. SAMUEL BUTLER

Life is an end in itself, and the only question as to whether it is worth living is whether you have had enough of it. DR OLIVER WENDELL HOLMES

Is life worth living? That depends on the liver. ANON

Litigant: Litigant. A person about to give up his skin for the hope of retaining his bones. AMBROSE BIERCE

Little: Sometimes when I consider what tremendous consequences come from little things, I am tempted to think that there are no little things. BRUCE BARTON

Longevity: No one is so old as to think he cannot live one more year. CICERO

Love: In women pity begets love, in men love begets pity. J. CHURTON COLLINS

Love endures only when the lovers love many things together and not merely each other. WALTER LIPPMAN

When love and skill work together – expect a masterpiece. ANON

Love is the quicksilver in the hand. Leave the fingers open, and it stays. Clutch it, and it darts away. ANON

Do not confuse the pleasure of pleasing with the happiness of loving. COCO CHANEL

Time is too slow for those who wait, too swift for those who fear, too long for those who grieve, too short for those who rejoice. But for those who love, time is not. HENRY VAN DYKE

The wise woman never gives her love, but lets it out at the highest rate of security. COUNT HENRI DE TOULOUSE-LAUTREC

Friendship is a disinterested commerce between equals; love, an abject intercourse between tyrants and slaves. OLIVER GOLDSMITH

To say that you can love one person all your life is just like saying that one candle will continue burning as long as you live. LEO TOLSTOY

There are two sorts of affection — the love for a woman you respect, and the love for a woman you love. SIR ARTHUR PINERO

Love is the history of a woman's life; it is an episode in man's. MADAME DE STAEL

Let me not to the marriage of true minds
Admit impediments. Love is not love
Which alters when it alteration finds. WILLIAM SHAKESPEARE

When one is in love one begins to deceive oneself. And one ends by deceiving others. OSCAR WILDE

Love does not consist in gazing at each other but in looking together in the same direction. ANTOINE DE SAINT-EXUPÉRY

First love is only a little foolishness and a lot of curiosity. GEORGE BERNARD SHAW

The magic of first love is our ignorance that it can ever end. BENJAMIN DISRAELI

Love is a disease which fills you with a desire to be desired. COUNT HENRI DE TOULOUSE-LAUTREC

The love of liberty is the love of others; the love of power is the love of ourselves. WILLIAM HAZLITT

One often passes from love to ambition; but rarely returns from ambition to love. FRANCOIS

Lover: One can be a soldier without dying, and a lover without sighing. SIR EDWIN ARNOLD

If ever a woman feels proud of her lover, it is when she sees him as a successful public speaker. HARRIET BEECHER STOWE

Machines: Machines are beneficial to the degree that they eliminate the need for labour, harmful to the degree that they eliminate the need for skill. ANON

One machine can do the work of fifty ordinary men. No machine can do the work of one extraordinary man. ELBERT HUBBARD

Man: Know then thyself, presume not God to scan,
The proper study of mankind is man. ALEXANDER POPE

The secret of a man who is universally interesting, is that he is universally interested. WILLIAM DEAN HOWELLS

Happy is the man with a wife to tell him what to do and a secretary to do it. LORD MANCROFT

The ultimate result of shielding men from the effects of folly, is to fill the world with fools. HERBERT SPENCER

Man to man: For years I saved for a rainy day. Then I met a girl who wiped it out with one monsoon.

The man who cannot live with himself, cannot live with anyone. ANON

No man is exempt from saying silly things. The misfortune is to say them painstakingly. MICHEL DE MONTAIGNE

The truly free man is he who knows how to decline a dinner invitation without giving an excuse. JULES RENARD

How a man plays the game shows something of his character; how he loses shows all of it. ANON

The most difficult secret for a man to keep is the opinion he has of himself. ANON

Whenever I meet a man who would make a good husband, he is. SPINSTER—ANON

No man is the whole of himself; his friends are the rest of him. ANON

Man's extremity is God's opportunity. JOHN FLAVEL

Speak well of your enemies, sir, you made them. OREN ARNOLD

I have found men more kind than I expected, and less just. SAMUEL JOHNSON

In other living creatures the ignorance of themselves is nature, but in men it is vice. BOETHIUS

Brutes never meet in bloody fray,
Nor cut each other's throats for pay. JONATHAN SWIFT

Human beings are the only animals of which I am thoroughly and cravenly afraid. GEORGE BERNARD SHAW

A man may be a fool and not know it — but not if he is married. H. L. MENCKEN

From each according to his abilities, to each according to his needs. KARL MARX

Only this distinguishes us from the other animals: we drink when we are not thirsty and we make love on the spur of the moment. PIERRE DE BEAUMARCHAIS

All creatures kill. There seems to be no exception. But of the whole list man is the only one that kills for fun; he is the only one that kills in malice, the only one that kills for revenge. MARK TWAIN

All the animals except man know that the principal business of life is to enjoy it. SAMUEL BUTLER

The propensity to truck, barter and exchange one thing for another . . . is common to all men, and to be found in no other race of animals. ADAM SMITH

Man is the only animal that laughs and weeps; for he is the only animal that is struck with the difference between what things are and what they might have been. WILLIAM HAZLITT

Mankind: Virtue in distress and vice in triumph make atheists of mankind. JOHN DRYDEN

He who surpasses or subdues mankind must look down on the hate of those below. LORD BYRON

Manners: There is a certain dignity of manners absolutely necessary to make even the most valuable character either respected or respectable. LORD CHESTERFIELD

Good manners are made up of petty sacrifices. RALPH WALDO EMERSON

Good breeding consists in concealing how much we think of ourselves and how little we think of the other person. MARK TWAIN

The society of women is the foundation of good manners. JOHANN WOLFGANG VON GOETHE

When a woman tells you her age, it's all right to look surprised, but don't scowl. WILSON MIZNER

Marriage: Let us embrace, and from this very moment vow an eternal misery together. THOMAS OTWAY

A woman marries a man with the ridiculous belief that she can change him; a man marries a woman with the naive idea that she will continue to be the same. LAURIE PEAK

Wife, about weary man of the house: 'He had a hard day at the office. The man he passes the buck to was out.'

A perfect wife is one who doesn't expect a perfect husband. ANON

The critical period in matrimony is breakfast time. ANON

It is always incomprehensible to a man that a woman should ever refuse an offer of marriage. JANE AUSTEN

Men marry because they are tired; women because they are curious; both are disappointed. OSCAR WILDE

Marriage always demands the greatest understanding of the art of insincerity possible between two human beings. VICKI BAUM

A marriage is likely to be called happy if neither party ever expected to get much happiness out of it. BERTRAND RUSSELL

It is a woman's business to get married as soon as possible, and a man's to keep unmarried as long as he can. GEORGE BERNARD SHAW

The trouble with marriage is that while every woman is at heart a mother, every man is at heart a bachelor. E. V. LUCAS

One was never married, and that's his hell; another is, and that's his plague. AMBROSE BIERCE

Here's to woman. Would that we could fall into her arms without falling into her hands. AMBROSE BIERCE

They dream in courtship, but in wedlock wake. ALEXANDER POPE

I am not against hasty marriages, where a mutual flame is fanned by an adequate income. WILKIE COLLINS

Every man plays the fool once in his life, but to marry is playing the fool all one's life long. WILLIAM CONGREVE

By all means marry; if you get a good wife you'll become happy; if you get a bad one, you'll become a philosopher. SOCRATES

He's a wise man who marries a harlot; he's on the surest side. Who but an ass would marry an uncertainty? THOMAS SHADWELL

Keep your eyes wide open before marriage, and half-shut afterwards. BENJAMIN FRANKLIN

Marriage is one long conversation, chequered by dispute. ROBERT LOUIS STEVENSON

Nowadays women don't hire domestic help – they marry it. EARL WILSON

Martyr: There have been quite as many martyrs for bad causes as for good ones. HENDRIK VAN LOON

A thing is not necessarily true because a man dies for it. OSCAR WILDE

Meetings: Few people know how to hold a meeting. Even fewer know how to let it go. ANON

Memory: To be wronged is nothing, unless you continue to remember it. CONFUCIUS

The moment may be temporary, but the memory is forever. ANON

Men: Men who do not make advances to women are apt to become victims to women who make advances to them. WALTER BAGEHOT

Mercy: A miscarriage of mercy is as much to be guarded against as a miscarriage of justice. ROBERT LYND

Middle age: You've reached middle age when all you exercise is caution. ANON

Middle class: The most perfect political community is one in which the middle class is in control and outnumbers both of the other classes. ARISTOTLE

Miracles: Miracles sometimes happen, but one has to work terribly hard for them. CHAIM WEIZMANN

Misery: I have always held firmly to the thought that each one of us can do a little to bring some portion of misery to an end. ALBERT SCHWEITZER

Mistress: Next to the pleasure of making a new mistress is that of being rid of an old one. WILLIAM WYCHERLEY

Moderate: Moderate: A fellow who makes enemies left and right.

Money: Before borrowing money from a friend, decide which you need more. ADDISON H. HALLOCK

When I was young I used to think that money was the most important thing in life; now that I am old, I know it is. OSCAR WILDE

There are few sorrows, however poignant, in which a good income is of no avail. LOGAN PEARSALL SMITH

If you would like to know the value of money, go and try to borrow some. BENJAMIN FRANKLIN

Moralize: A man who moralizes is usually a hypocrite, and a woman who moralizes is invariably plain. OSCAR WILDE

Mothers: God could not be everywhere and therefore he made mothers. JEWISH PROVERB

Motive: Never ascribe to an opponent motives meaner than your own. SIR J. M. BARRIE

Motoring: Traffic warning sign: 'Heads you win – cocktails you lose.'

Music: Music expresses that which cannot be put into words and that which cannot remain silent. VICTOR HUGO

National Debt: Public credit means contracting of debts which a nation can never pay. WILLIAM COBBETT

Nations: No nation is so poor that it cannot afford free speech. DANIEL MOYNIHAM

Newspaper: A newspaper is not just for reporting the news as it is, but to make people angry enough to do something about it. ANON

I fear three newspapers more than a hundred thousand bayonets. NAPOLEON BONAPARTE

Obstinacy: The difference between perseverance and obstinacy is that perseverence means a strong will and obstinacy means a strong won't. ANON

Old age: When people tell you how young you look, they are also telling you how old you are. CARY GRANT

Oneself: Since all future is concealed from sight, I need but strive to make the next step right. ELLA WHEELER WILCOX

Opinion: There's a difference between opinion and conviction. My opinion is something that is true for me personally. My conviction is something that is true for everybody – in my opinion. SYLVIA CORDWOOD

Opinion is holding something to be provisionally true which you do not know to be false. SAINT BERNARD

Opinions have vested interests just as men have. SAMUEL BUTLER

Opportunities: Weak men wait for opportunities; strong men take them. ANON

Optimist: Optimist: A bridegroom who thinks he has no bad habits. ANON

An optimist is a man who waits in his car with the engine running, while his wife goes shopping. ANON

Optimists and pessimists have one fault in common; they're both afraid of the truth. ANON

An optimist is wrong as often as a pessimist, but he has much more fun. ANON

Keep your face toward the sunshine, and the shadows will fall behind you. M. B. WHITMAN

An optimist is a guy who has never had much experience. DON MARQUIS

An optimist is a fellow who believes what's going to be will be postponed. F. McKINNEY HUBBARD

Orgy: He who makes a beast of himself gets rid of the pain of being a man. SAMUEL JOHNSON

Originality: As usual the Liberals offer a mixture of sound and original ideas. Unfortunately none of the sound ideas is original and none of the original is sound. HAROLD MACMILLAN

Originality is a thing we constantly clamour for, and constantly quarrel with. THOMAS CARLYLE

Pacification: The full potentialities of human fury cannot be reached until a friend of both parties tactfully intervenes. G. K. CHESTERTON

Am I not destroying my enemies when I make friends of them? ABRAHAM LINCOLN

Those who in quarrels interpose,
Must often wipe a bloody nose. JOHN GAY

Painting: Modern paintings are like women. You'll never enjoy them if you try to understand them. ANON

Parents: Parents spend the first part of a child's life getting him to walk and talk, and the rest of his childhood getting him to sit down and shut up. ANON

Children aren't happy with nothing to ignore.
And that's what parents were created for. OGDEN NASH

Reasoning with a child is fine, if you can reach the child's reason without destroying your own. JOHN MASON BROWN

Parliament: Of all the puppet-shows in the Satanic Carnival of the Earth, the most contemptible puppet-show is a Parliament with a mob pulling the strings. JOHN RUSKIN

Party: To sacrifice one's honour to one's party is so unselfish an act that our most generous statesmen have not hesitated to do it. LORD DARLING

Patience: Patience is bitter, but its fruit is sweet. ANON

How poor are they that have not patience:
What wound did ever heal but by degrees. WILLIAM SHAKESPEARE

Patriotism: Patriotism is your conviction that this country is superior to all others because you were born in it. GEORGE BERNARD SHAW

Our country right or wrong. When right, to be kept right; when wrong, to be put right. CARL SCHURZ

The proper means of increasing the love we bear our native country is to reside some time in a foreign one. WILLIAM SHENSTONE

Patriotism is the last refuge of a scoundrel. SAMUEL JOHNSON

Where liberty dwells, there is my country. ATTRIBUTED TO: THOMAS JEFFERSON AND THOMAS PAINE

I tremble for my country when I reflect that God is just. THOMAS JEFFERSON

I realise that patriotism is not enough. I must have no hatred or bitterness towards anyone. EDITH CAVELL

Patronage: The penalty of success is to be bored by the attentions of people who formerly snubbed you. MARY W. LITTLE

Peace: More than an end to war, we want an end to the beginnings of all wars. FRANKLIN D. ROOSEVELT

Pedigree: Englishmen hate Liberty and Equality too much to understand them. But every Englishman loves a pedigree. GEORGE BERNARD SHAW

Pension: I advise you to go on living solely to enrage those who are paying your annuities. It is the only pleasure I have left. VOLTAIRE

People: Much of the good work of the world has been that of dull people who have done their best. ANON

Most people would rather defend to the death your right to say it than listen to it. ANON

People who want by the yard but try by the inch, should be kicked by the foot. ANON

People who bite the hand that feeds them usually lick the boots that kick them. ANON

People who value their privileges above their principles soon lose both. DWIGHT D. EISENHOWER

When we are alone, we have our thoughts to watch; when we are in the family, our tempers; and when in society, our tongues. CHARLES KINGSLEY

Most people commit the same mistake with God that they do with their friends; they do all the talking. ANON

We do not love people so much for the good they have done us, as for the good we have done them. LEO TOLSTOY

Most people repent of their sins by thanking God they ain't so wicked as their neighbours. JOSH BILLINGS

We may not return the affection of those who like us, but we always respect their good judgement. ANON

Perfection: Seek not every quality in one individual. CONFUCIUS

Perfume: Scent announces a woman's arrival and delays her departure. ANON

Persistence: Take care to get what you like or you will be forced to like what you get. GEORGE BERNARD SHAW

Pessimism: I have never seen pessimism in a Company prospectus. SIR WILLIAM CONNOR

Pessimist: A pessimist is one who has been intimately acquainted with an optimist. ELBERT HUBBARD

Do you know what a pessimist is? A man who thinks everybody as nasty as himself, and hates them for it. GEORGE BERNARD SHAW

Pets: The great pleasure of a dog is that you may make a fool of yourself with him and not only will he not scold you, but he will make a fool of himself too. SAMUEL BUTLER

Well-washed and well-combed domestic pets grow dull; they miss the stimulus of fleas. SIR FRANCIS GALTON

When I play with my cat, who knows whether she is not amusing herself with me more than I with her. MICHEL DE MONTAIGNE

A dog teaches a boy fidelity, perseverance, and to turn round three times before lying down. ROBERT BENCHLEY

Philanthropists: The luxury of doing good surpasses every other personal enjoyment. JOHN GAY

Philanthropy is the refuge of people who wish to annoy their fellow creatures. OSCAR WILDE

Philosophy: Unintelligible answers to insoluble problems. HENRY ADAMS

When he who hears doesn't know what he who speaks means, and when he who speaks doesn't know what he himself means — that is Philosophy. VOLTAIRE

All are lunatics, but he who can analyse his delusions is called a philosopher. AMBROSE BIERCE

Pity: Pity costs nothing, and 'aint worth nothing. JOSH BILLINGS

Platitude: All that is mortal of a departed truth. AMBROSE BIERCE

Poet: A poet is someone who is astonished by everything. ANON

Sir, I admit your general rule,
That every poet is a fool.
But you yourself may serve to show it,
That every fool is not a poet. SAMUEL TAYLOR COLERIDGE

Poetry: Poetry is a mixture of common sense, which not all have, with an uncommon sense, which very few have. JOHN MASEFIELD

Poetry is the journal of a sea animal living on land, wanting to fly in the air. CARL SANDBURG

Politeness: Politeness is good nature regulated by good sense. SYDNEY SMITH

Politeness is to human nature what warmth is to wax. ANON

Politicians: Exhortation to do something is the last resort of politicians who are at a loss to know what to do themselves. SIR PAUL CHAMBERS

The most successful politician is he who says what everybody is thinking most often and in the loudest voice. THEODORE ROOSEVELT

A politician is an arse upon which everyone has sat except a man. E. E. CUMMINGS

It is easier to appear worthy of a position one does not hold, than of the office which one fills. FRANCOIS

The punishment which the wise suffer who refuse to take part in the government is, to live under the government of worse men. PLATO

A lot of politicians make the mistake of forgetting that they've been appointed instead of anointed. ANON

When politicians appeal to all intelligent voters, they mean everyone who is going to vote for them. FRANKLIN P. ADAMS

When a politician says: 'We're all in the same boat', he usually means he wants to play Captain while the rest of us do the rowing.

Politics: A government that robs Peter to pay Paul can always depend on the support of Paul. GEORGE BERNARD SHAW

Politics is like roller skating. You go partly where you want to go, and partly where the damned things take you. HENRY FOUNTAIN ASHURST

Politics are now nothing more than a means of rising in the world. SAMUEL JOHNSON

Any party which takes credit for the rain must not be surprised if its opponents blame it for the drought. DWIGHT W. MORROW

D'ye think that statesmen's kindnesses proceed from any principles but their own need? SIR ROBERT HOWARD

Cease being the slave of a political party and you become its deserter. JULES SIMON

The more you listen to political speeches, the more you realize that ours is indeed a land of promise. ANON

Politics is the science of how who gets what, when and why? SIDNEY HILLMAN

Policy: Lines of least resistance make crooked rivers and crooked men. WILLIAM H. DANFORTH

No foreign policy – no matter how ingenious, has any chance of success if it is born in the minds of a few and carried in the hearts of none. HENRY KISSINGER

Poverty: Poverty is no disgrace to a man, but it is confoundly inconvenient. SYDNEY SMITH

A good poor man is better than a good rich man because he has to resist more temptations. PLATO

Poverty keeps together more homes than it breaks up. H. H. MUNRO

Poverty does not mean the possession of little, but the lack of much. ANTIPATER OF MACEDONIA

In wealth many friends, in poverty not even relations. ANON

No man should commend poverty unless he is poor. SAINT BERNARD

I used to think I was poor. Then they told me I wasn't poor, I was needy. Then they told me it was self-defeating to think of myself as needy, I was deprived. Then they told me deprived was a bad image, I was underprivileged. Then they told me underprivileged was overused, I was disadvantaged. I still don't have a dime. But I sure have a great vocabulary. JULES FEIFFER

It is easier to praise poverty than bear it. ANON

Power: Power tends to corrupt, and absolute power corrupts absolutely. Great men are almost always bad men. LORD ACTON

To have a great man for a friend seems pleasant to those who have never tried it; those who have, fear it. HORACE

A continual feast of commendation is only to be attained by merit or by wealth. SAMUEL JOHNSON

No government has ever combined so passionate a lust for power with such incurable impotence in its exercise. SIR WINSTON CHURCHILL

You cannot have power for good without having power for evil too. Even mother's milk nourishes murderers as well as heroes. GEORGE BERNARD SHAW

Praise: He who praises everybody praises nobody. SAMUEL JOHNSON

Preaching: A preacher should ask himself – am I about to preach because I want to say something, or because I have something to say? ANON

Precaution: It is best to read the weather forecasts before we pray for rain. MARK TWAIN

Prejudice: A prejudice is a vagrant opinion without visible means of support. ANON

Prejudices are the chains forged by ignorance to keep men apart. COUNTESS OF BLESSINGTON

Prejudice is a great time saver. You can form opinions without having to get the facts. ANON

Principles: When you say that you agree to a thing in principle you mean that you have not the slightest intention of carrying it out in practice. ANON

Problems: Drowning problems in an ocean of information is not the same as solving them. RAY BROWN

There's only one way to solve all the economic problems of the Country. Make complacency taxable. ANON

Every problem has a solution. If there is no solution it's a fact. And if a fact, accept it. ANON

Profession: We must hold a man amenable to reason for the choice of his daily craft or profession. It is not an excuse any longer for his deeds that they are the custom of his trade. What business has he with an evil trade. RALPH WALDO EMERSON

Profits: It is a Socialist idea that making profits is a vice. I consider the real vice is making losses. SIR WINSTON CHURCHILL

Progress: You can't say that civilisation don't advance, for in every war they kill you a new way. WILL ROGERS

Progress is impossible without change; and those who cannot change their minds cannot change anything. GEORGE BERNARD SHAW

Remember the turtle progresses only when he sticks out his neck. ANON

Progress might have been all right once, but it has gone on too long. ANON

All progress is based upon a universal innate desire on the part of every organism to live beyond its income. SAMUEL BUTLER

Promises: Half the promises people say were never kept, were never made. E. W. HOWE

Property: Thieves respect property. They merely wish the property to become their property that they may more perfectly respect it. G. K. CHESTERTON

Prophecy: Prophecy is the most gratuitous form of error. GEORGE ELIOT

Our grand business is undoubtedly not to see what lies dimly at a distance, but to do what lies clearly at hand. THOMAS CARLYLE

Tomorrow's fate, though thou be wise,
Thou canst not tell, nor yet surmise:
Pass, therefore, not today in vain,
For it will never come again. OMAR KHAYYAM

Of all the horrid, hideous notes of woe,
Is that portentous phrase, 'I told you so.' LORD BYRON

Protest: A fellow who is always declaring he's no fool usually has his suspicions. WILSON MIZNER

Proverb: A proverb is the wisdom of many and the wit of one. LORD JOHN RUSSELL

Provocation: A man never tells you anything until you contradict him. GEORGE BERNARD SHAW

Public Office: Holding public office is like trying to dance in a Night Club. No matter what you do, you rub somebody the wrong way. ANON

Public Opinion: Public opinion, a vulgar, impertinent, anonymous tyrant who deliberately makes life unpleasant for anyone who is not content to be the average man. DEAN W. R. INGE

Public opinion, an attempt to organize the ignorance of the community and to elevate it to the dignity of physical force. OSCAR WILDE

Public Speaking: Many a man's tongue broke his nose. SEUMAS MACMANUS

Puritan: The puritan through Life's sweet garden goes,
       To pluck the thorn and cast away the rose. ANON

Quotations: I hate quotations. RALPH WALDO EMERSON

Rain: The good rain, like a bad preacher, does not know when to leave off. RALPH WALDO EMERSON

Reading: Reading is sometimes an ingenious device for avoiding thought. SIR ARTHUR HELPS

Realisation: After the age of 45 one realises that youth is wasted on the young. ANON

Reason: The only reason some people listen to reason is to gain time for rebuttal. ANON

Nothing has an uglier look to us than reason when it is not on our side. LORD HALIFAX

It is useless for us to attempt to reason a man out of a thing he has never been reasoned into. JONATHAN SWIFT

Reason is our soul's left hand, Faith her right;
By these we reach divinity. JOHN DONNE

Recognition: If we had no faults we should not take so much pleasure in noticing them in others. FRANCOIS

Recreation: Public money is scarcely ever so well employed as in securing bits of waste ground and keeping them as open spaces. SIR ARTHUR HELPS

References: The hardest thing is writing a recommendation for someone we know. F. McKINNEY HUBBARD

Reform: Those who are fond of setting things to rights have no great objection to seeing them wrong. WILLIAM HAZLITT

Treason doth never prosper; What's
the reason?
For if it prosper, none dare call
it treason. SIR JOHN HARRINGTON

Every reform is only a mask under cover of which a more terrible reform, which dare not yet name itself, advances. RALPH WALDO EMERSON

Refusal: It is kindness to refuse immediately what you intend to deny. PUBLILIUS SYRUS 43BC

Reliable: It is the dull man who is always sure, and the sure man who is always dull. H. L. MENCKEN

Religion: All religions are founded on the fear of the many and the cleverness of the few. STENDHAL

Formal religion was organized for slaves: it offered them consolation which Earth did not provide. ELBERT HUBBARD

Men despise religion; they hate it, and fear it is true. BLAISE PASCAL

When Satan makes impure verses, Allah sends a divine tune to cleanse them. GEORGE BERNARD SHAW

There is no higher religion than the truth. ANON

Science without religion is lame: religion without science is blind. ALBERT EINSTEIN

The devil can cite Scripture for his purpose. WILLIAM SHAKESPEARE

Men never do evil so completely and cheerfully as when they do it from religious conviction. BLAISE PASCAL

How else but through a broken heart may Lord Christ enter in? OSCAR WILDE

When I'm in health I'm not at all religious. But when I'm sick I'm very religious. BRENDAN BEHAN

Remorse: For the sins ye do by two and two ye must pay for one by one. RUDYARD KIPLING

Re-organize: We tend to meet any new situation by re-organizing; and a wonderful method it can be for creating the illusion of progress while producing confusion, inefficiency and demoralization. PETRONIUS ARBITER

Reputation: You can't build a reputation on what you are going to do. ANON

Conscience and reputation are two things. Conscience is due to yourself, reputation to your neighbour. SAINT AUGUSTINE

The great difficulty is first to win a reputation; the next to keep it while you live; and the next to preserve it after you die. BENJAMIN HAYDON

The fame of great men ought always to be estimated by the means used to acquire it. FRANCOIS

To enjoy a good reputation, give publicly, and steal privately. JOSH BILLINGS

Character is much easier kept than recovered. THOMAS PAINE

How many people live on the reputation of the reputation they might have made. DR OLIVER WENDELL HOLMES

Responsibilities: It is easy to dodge our responsibilities, but we cannot dodge the consequences of dodging our responsibilities. ANON

Few things help an individual more than to place responsibility upon him and to let him know you trust him. ANON

Woman to friend: 'I never vote. It's such a relief not to feel responsible for anything that happens in Parliament.'

It is our responsibilities, not ourselves that we should take seriously. PETER USTINOV

To gain one's way is no escape from the responsibility for an inferior solution. SIR WINSTON CHURCHILL

The most anxious man in a prison is the Governor. GEORGE BERNARD SHAW

Retirement: Retirement takes all the fun out of Saturdays. ANON

Retribution: Retribution often means that we eventually do to ourselves what we have done to others. ANON

Revenge: A man that studieth revenge keeps his own wounds green. FRANCIS BACON

Revolution: A populace never rebels from passion for attack, but from impatience of suffering. EDMUND BURKE

Inferiors revolt in order that they may be equal, and equals that they be superior. Such is the state of mind which creates revolution. ARISTOTLE

Revolutions have never lightened the burden of tyranny; they have only shifted it to another shoulder. GEORGE BERNARD SHAW

Riches: The rich never feel so good as when they are speaking of their possessions as responsibilities. ROBERT LYND

He that maketh haste to be rich shall not be innocent. BIBLE —PROVERBS

To suppose, as we all suppose, that we could be rich and not behave as the rich behave, is like supposing that we could drink all day and stay sober. LOGAN PEARSALL SMITH

The greatest luxury of riches is that they enable you to escape so much good advice. The rich are always advising the poor, but the poor seldom venture to return the compliment. SIR ARTHUR HELPS

Rights: The law often allows what honour forbids. WILLIAM SAUBIN

Romance: Romance like a ghost, eludes touching. It is always where you were, not where you are. G. W. CURTIS

Royalty: The fortune which made you a king, forbade you to have a friend. JUNIUS

Rumour: All who told it added something new,
　　　　　And all who heard it made enlargements too.
　　　　　ALEXANDER POPE

Saints: The way of this world is to praise dead saints and persecute living ones. NATHANIEL HOWE

Salvation: He who created us without our help will not save us without our consent. SAINT AUGUSTINE

Satire: Satire is the art of stepping on somebody's toes so that he feels it but doesn't yell. ANON

Secretary: Secretary on telephone: 'Our automatic answering device is away for repairs – this is a person speaking.'

Secrets: Keep a secret, it's your slave. Tell it, and it's your master. ANON

Some people's idea of keeping a secret is lowering their voices when they tell it. ANON

Self-denial: Self-denial is not a virtue; it is only the effect of prudence on rascality. GEORGE BERNARD SHAW

Self-esteem: Perhaps the only true dignity of man is his capacity to despise himself. GEORGE SANTAYANA

Self-love: People fall in love with themselves almost immediately after birth. This is invariably the beginning of a life-long romance. There is no record of infidelity, separation, or divorce between humans and their egos. HARRY SINGER

Self-pity: A capacity for self-pity is one of the last things that any woman surrenders. IRVIN S. COBB

Self-respect: No man who is occupied in doing a very difficult thing, and doing it very well, ever loses his self-respect. GEORGE BERNARD SHAW

Sentimentality: Is no indication of a warm heart; nothing weeps more copiously than a chunk of ice. ANON

Sermon: You can preach a better sermon with your life than with your lips. OLIVER GOLDSMITH

Silence: He approaches nearest to the gods who knows how to be silent, even though he is in the right. CATO

An inability to stay quiet is one of the most conspicuous failings of mankind. WALTER BAGEIIOT

Most of us know how to say nothing. Few of us know when. ANON

Keep quiet and people will think you a philosopher. LATIN PROVERB

Silence is the unbearable repartee. ANON

Simplicity: Everything should be made as simple as possible, but not simpler. ALBERT EINSTEIN

Sin: To abstain from sin when a man cannot sin is to be forsaken by sin, not to forsake it. SAINT AUGUSTINE

He that falls into sin is a man; that grieves at it, is a saint; that boasteth of it, is a devil. THOMAS FULLER

Sincerity: People are always sincere. They change sincerities, that's all. TRISTAN BERNARD

A little sincerity is a dangerous thing, and a great deal of it is absolutely fatal. OSCAR WILDE

Sincerity resembles a spice. Too much repels you and too little leaves you wanting. BILL COPELAND

Slander: It takes your enemy and your friend, working together, to hurt you to the heart: the one to slander you, and the other to get the news to you. MARK TWAIN

Sleep: All men whilst they are awake are in one common world: but each one of them, when he is asleep, is in a world of his own. PLUTARCH

Smile: A smile costs less than electricity and gives more light. SCOTTISH PROVERB

Snoring: Laugh and the world laughs with you: snore and you sleep alone. ANON

Sobriety: What soberness conceals drunkenness reveals. LATIN PROVERB

Socialism: When I was young I thought Socialism was the mathematics of justice. Now I realise it is only the arithmetic of envy. MARTIN COLLINS

Essentially Socialism is no more and no less a criticism of the idea of property in the light of the public good. H. G. WELLS

Society: Teach the English how to talk and the Irish how to listen; then society will be quite civilised. ANON

I'll take heaven for the climate and hell for society. MARK TWAIN

I had three chairs in my house: one for solitude, two for friendship, three for society. HENRY DAVID THOREAU

Solitude: I never found the companion that was so companionable as solitude. HENRY DAVID THOREAU

Soul: The soul too, has her virginity and must bleed a little before bearing fruit. GEORGE SANTAYANA

Soviet Russia: It is true that liberty is precious — so precious that it must be rationed. LENIN

Speaker: Toast master to assembled groups: 'Our next speaker needs no introduction. He changed his mind and stayed at home.'

He can best be described as one of those orators who, before they get up, do not know what they are going to say; when they are speaking, do not know what they are saying; and, when they have sat down, do not know what they have said. SIR WINSTON CHURCHILL

Adepts in the speaking trade,
Keep a cough by them ready made. CHARLES CHURCHILL

What orators lack in depth they make up to you in length. CHARLES DE MONTESQUIEU

Speeches: It usually takes more than three weeks to prepare a good impromptu speech. MARK TWAIN

Speak when you're angry and you will make the best speech you will ever regret. ANON

A speech is like a love affair. Any fool can start one, but to end it tidily requires considerable skill. ANON

I do not object to people looking at their watches when I am speaking. But I strongly object when they start shaking them to make certain they are still going. LORD BIRKETT

A wise speech sleeps in a foolish ear. EURIPEDES

Stability: Stability is not immobility. METTERNICH

State: While the state exists there is no freedom: when there is freedom there will be no state. LENIN

I look upon an increase in the powers of the State with the greatest fear, because, although while apparently doing good by minimizing exploitation, it does the greatest harm to mankind by destroying individuality, which lies at the root of all progress. MAHATMA GHANDI

Statesmen: A politician thinks of the next election; a statesman, of the next generation. JAMES FREEMAN CLARKE

A constitutional statesman is in general a man of common opinions and uncommon abilities. WALTER BAGEHOT

Statistics: Statistics are like alienists – they will testify for either side. FIORELLO LA GUARDIA

Stature: A man of stature has no need of status. ANON

Status Symbols: Status symbols are medals you buy yourself. ANON

It is the superfluous things for which men sweat. SENECA

Strength: The weak have one weapon: the errors of those who think they are strong. GEORGES BIDAULT

Suburbia: Heaven is not built of country seats,
But little queer suburban streets.
CHRISTOPHER MORLEY

Success: The secret of success in life is known only to those who have not succeeded. J. CHURTON COLLINS

Let us be thankful for fools. But for them the rest of us could not succeed. MARK TWAIN

The common idea that success spoils people by making them vain, egotistic, and self-complacent is erroneous; on the contrary, it makes them, for the most part, humble, tolerant, and kind. Failure makes people cruel and bitter. W. SOMERSET MAUGHAM

For a hundred that can bear adversity there is hardly one that can bear prosperity. THOMAS CARLYLE

All you need in this life is ignorance and confidence, and then success is sure. MARK TWAIN

There is always something about your success that displeases even your best friends. OSCAR WILDE

Success is what gives us the confidence to put into practice what failure has taught us. PABLO CARRASCO

Success. The only infallible criterion of wisdom to vulgar judgement. EDMUND BURKE

Suicide: There are many who dare not kill themselves for fear of what the neighbours will say. CYRIL CONNOLLY

SUICIDE

It is always consoling to think of suicide: in that way one gets through many a bad night. FRIEDRICH NIETZSCHE

It is the role of cowardice, not of courage, to crouch in a hole, under a massive tomb, to avoid the blows of fortune. MICHEL DE MONTAIGNE

Superiority: My family pride is something inconceivable. I can't help it. I was born sneering. SIR W. S. GILBERT

People of quality know everything without learning anything. MOLIÈRE

Superstition: Superstition is the religion of feeble minds. EDMUND BURKE

Tact: Tact is the rare ability to keep silent while two friends are arguing, and you know both of them are wrong. ANON

Never claim as a right what you can ask as a favour. J. CHURTON COLLINS

Tact consists in knowing how far we may go too far. JEAN COCTEAU

Take: Take what you want, said God; take it and pay for it. OLD SPANISH PROVERB

Talent: Use what talents you have; the woods would have little music if no birds sang their song except those who sang best. ANON

Taxation: The art of taxation consists in so plucking the goose as to obtain the largest amount of feathers with the least amount of hissing. JEAN BAPTISTE COLBERT

Teach: To teach is to learn twice. JOSEPH JOUBERT

Teacher: The vanity of teaching often tempts a man to forget he is a blockhead. GEORGE SAVILE

He who can, does. He who cannot, teaches. GEORGE BERNARD SHAW

Everybody who is incapable of learning has taken to teaching. OSCAR WILDE

Technicians: There are three ways of courting ruin — women, gambling and calling in technicians. GEORGE POMPIDOU

Temptation: A compulsion is a highbrow term for a temptation we're not trying too hard to resist. ANON

Resisting temptation is easier when you think you'll probably get another chance later on. ANON

There are several good protections against temptation but the surest is cowardice. MARK TWAIN

The resolution to avoid an evil is seldom framed till the evil is so far advanced as to make avoidance impossible. THOMAS HARDY

The only way to get rid of temptation is to yield to it. OSCAR WILDE

The last temptation is the greatest treason. To do the right deed for the wrong reason. T. S. ELIOT

Theology: Theology is the effort to explain the unknowable in terms of the not worth knowing. H. L. MENCKEN

Thinking: Thinking is like loving and dying. Each of us must do it for himself. JOSIA ROYCE

A great many people think they are thinking when they are merely rearranging their prejudices. WILLIAM JAMES

Thrifty: How easy it is for a man to die rich, if he will but be contented to live miserable. HENRY FIELDING

Time: Time is money and many people pay their debts with it. JOSH BILLINGS

How you spend your time is more important than how you spend your money. Money mistakes can be corrected, but time is gone for ever. DAVID NORRIS

Time: that which man is always trying to kill, but which ends in killing him. HERBERT SPENCER

Tobacco: I kissed my first woman and smoked my first cigarette on the same day; I have never had time for tobacco since. ARTURO TOSCANINI

Today: It is a mistake to look too far ahead. Only one link in the chain of destiny can be handled at a time. SIR WINSTON CHURCHILL

Tolerance: Tolerance: the suspicion that the other fellow might be right. ANON

Suffer fools gladly; they might be right. HOLBROOK JACKSON

Toleration: To tolerate everything is to teach nothing. DR F. J. KINSMAN

Tourist: The British tourist is always happy abroad as long as the natives are waiters. ROBERT MORLEY

Don't imagine I regard foreigners as inferior – they fascinate me. HAROLD WILSON

Travel: The man who goes alone can start today; but he who travels with another must wait till that other is ready. HENRY DAVID THOREAU

And let him go where he will, he can only find so much beauty or worth as he carries. RALPH WALDO EMERSON

A man travels all over the world in search of what he needs, and returns home to find it. ANON

Treason: Treason is loved of many, but the traitor hated of all. ROBERT GREENE

Treasury: In general, the art of government consists in taking as much money as possible from one party of the citizens to give it to the other. VOLTAIRE

Troubles: He that seeks trouble, it were a pity he should miss it. ENGLISH PROVERB

There's one thing to be said for inviting trouble; it usually accepts. ANON

Trust: We are inclined to believe those whom we do not know because they have never deceived us. SAMUEL JOHNSON

Better to trust the man who is frequently in error than the one who is never in doubt. ANON

Truth: I speak truth, not so much as I would, but as much as I dare; and I dare a little the more, as I grow older. MICHEL DE MONTAIGNE

Men occasionally stumble over the truth, but most of them pick themselves up and hurry off as if nothing had happened. SIR WINSTON CHURCHILL

It is always the best policy to speak the truth, unless, of course, you are an exceptionally good liar. JEROME K. JEROME

If you tell the truth you don't have to remember anything. MARK TWAIN

Listening to both sides of a story will convince you that there is more to a story than both sides. ANON

Keep raising the roof and people will think there's something wrong in your attic. FRANKLIN JONES

The most gleaming trophy a great man can claim is the discovery of a few truths and the destruction of a few errors. FREDERICK THE GREAT

When we stretch the truth, people usually see through it. ANON

Most of the changes we think we see in life are due to truths being in and out of favour. ANON

The truth shall make ye free, but first it shall make ye miserable. ANON

One of the hardest things to teach a child is that the truth is more important than the consequences. O. A. BATTISTA

Telling the truth to people who misunderstand you is generally promoting falsehood. SIR ANTHONY HOPE HAWKINS

To become properly acquainted with a truth we must first have disbelieved it, and disputed against it. PRINCE OTTO VON BISMARK

A man may be in just possession of truth as of a city, and yet be forced to surrender. SIR THOMAS BROWNE

He said true things, but called them by wrong names. ROBERT BROWNING

Unattainable: The indefatigable pursuit of an unattainable perfection even though it consists in nothing more than in the pounding of an old piano, is what alone gives a meaning to our lives on this unavailing star. LOGAN PEARSALL SMITH

Understanding: I make it a rule to only believe what I understand. BENJAMIN DISRAELI

Mockery ends where understanding begins. MARIE VON EBNER ESCHENBACH

University: A university should be a place of light, of liberty, and of learning. BENJAMIN DISRAELI

With one or two exceptions, colleges expect their players of games to be reasonably literate. SIR MAURICE BOWRA

'Tis well enough for a servant to be bred at university; but the education is a little too pedantic for a gentleman. WILLIAM CONGREVE

Unreasonable: It is folly to expect men to do all that they may reasonably be expected to do. RICHARD WHATELY

Untidiness: Chaos often breeds life, when order breeds habit. HENRY B. ADAMS

Vanity: The vanity of being known to be entrusted with a secret, is generally one of the chief motives to disclose it. SAMUEL JOHNSON

Vanity is the result of a delusion that someone is paying attention. ANON

Vanity dies hard; in some obstinate cases it outlives the man. ROBERT LOUIS STEVENSON

He makes people pleased with him by making them first pleased with themselves. LORD CHESTERFIELD

Vice: By virtue we merely mean the avoidance of the vices that do not attract us. ROBERT LYND

Virginity: One of the superstitions of the human mind is to suppose that virginity could be a virtue. VOLTAIRE

Virtue: What is virtue but the Trade Unionism of the married? GEORGE BERNARD SHAW

The resistance of a woman is not always proof of her virtue but more frequently of her experience. NINAN DE LENCLOS

What most people consider as virtue after the age of 40 is simply a loss of energy. ANON

Vow: When two people are under the influence of the most violent, most insane, most delusive, and most transient of passions, they are required to swear that they will remain in that excited, abnormal, and exhausting condition continuously until death do them part. GEORGE BERNARD SHAW

War: The more destructive war becomes the more fascinating we find it. GEORGE BERNARD SHAW

What we have gained by the war is, in one word, all that we should have lost without it. WILLIAM PITT

I gave my life for freedom — this I know:
For those who bade me fight had told me so. W. N. EWER

Wealth: Wealth is not his that has it, but his who enjoys it. ANON

But Satan now is wiser than of yore,
And tempts by making rich, not making poor. ALEXANDER POPE

If you can actually count your money then you are not really a rich man. PAUL GETTY

Wealth is not without its advantages and the case to the contrary, although it has often been made, has never proved widely persuasive. JOHN K. GALBRAITH

God shows his contempt for wealth by the kind of person he selects to receive it. AUSTIN O'MALLEY

Wedding: If it were not for the presents, an elopement would be preferable. GEORGE ADE

Whining: Those who do not complain are never pitied. JANE AUSTEN

Wickedness: Wickedness is a myth invented by good people to account for the curious attractiveness of others. OSCAR WILDE

Widow: Widows are divided into two classes – the bereaved and relieved. ANON

No crafty widows shall approach my bed:
They are too wise for bachelors to wed. ALEXANDER POPE

Wife: Never take for a wife a woman who has no faults. ANON

When a wife reminds a husband that they're not getting any younger, he can assume that she is about to suggest something expensive. ANON

The road to success is filled with women pushing their husbands along. LORD DEWAR

I chose my wife, as she did her wedding gown, not for a fine glossy surface, but such qualities as would wear well. OLIVER GOLDSMITH

He will hold thee, when his passion shall
    have spent its novel force,
Something better than his dog, a little
    dearer than his horse. LORD TENNYSON

A man likes his wife to be just clever enough to comprehend his cleverness, and just stupid enough to admire it. ISRAEL ZANGWILL

The man who waits to make an entirely reasonable will dies intestate. GEORGE BERNARD SHAW

Will-power: One real test of will-power is to have the same ailment someone is describing – and not mention it. ANON

Wisdom: If you can find a path with no obstacles, it probably doesn't lead anywhere. ANON

If you understand everything, you must be misinformed. JAPANESE PROVERB

You cannot expect a person to see eye to eye with you when you're looking down on him. ANON

Wisdom is knowing when you cannot be wise. ANON

Dig a well before you are thirsty. CHINESE PROVERB

There are two ways to get to the top of an oak tree – you can climb it or you can sit on an acorn. ANON

Wise men learn more from fools, than fools do from wise men. ANON

Philosophers have attempted to interpret the world, when what matters is to change it. KARL MARX

Wise people think all they say; fools say all they think. ANON

Give me beauty in the inward soul; for outward beauty I'm not likely to have. May I reckon the wise to be wealthy, and those who need the least to be most like the Gods. SOCRATES

The road of excess leads to the palace of wisdom. WILLIAM BLAKE

Wit: True wit is nature to advantage dress'd;
    What oft was thought, but ne'er so well expressed.
    ALEXANDER POPE

Woman: Heaven has no rage like love to
        hatred turned.
        Nor hell a fury like a woman scorned.
    WILLIAM CONGREVE

In all the woes that curse our race,
There is a lady in the case. SIR W. S. GILBERT

The only way for a woman to provide for herself decently is for her to be good to some man that can afford to be good to her. GEORGE BERNARD SHAW

The fundamental fault of the female character is that it has no sense of justice. ARTHUR SCHOPENHAUER

A woman can be anything that the man who loves her would have her to be. SIR J. M. BARRIE

Woman begins by resisting a man's advances and ends by blocking his retreat. OSCAR WILDE

When a woman behaves like a man why doesn't she behave like a nice man? DAME EDITH EVANS

There is only one real tragedy in a woman's life. The fact that her past is always her lover, and her future invariably her husband. OSCAR WILDE

If to her share some female errors fall,
Look on her face, and you'll forget them all. ALEXANDER POPE

It is often woman who inspires us with the great things that she will prevent us from accomplishing. ALEXANDRE DUMAS

A woman with true charm is one who can make a youth feel mature, an old man youthful, and a middle-aged man completely sure of himself. ANON

A woman will always sacrifice herself if you give her the opportunity. It is her favourite form of self-indulgence. W. SOMERSET MAUGHAN

To be happy with a man you must understand him a lot and love him a little. To be happy with a woman you must love her a lot and not try to understand her at all. HELEN ROWLAND

A man is as good as he has to be, and a woman as bad as she dares. ELBERT HUBBARD

A man is as old as he's feeling, a woman as old as she looks. MORTIMER COLLINS

A woman must choose: with a man liked by women, she is not sure; with a man disliked by women, she is not happy. ANATOLE FRANCE

Women: For a man to pretend to understand women is bad manners; for him really to understand them is bad morals. HENRY JAMES

The happiest women, like the happiest nations, have no history. GEORGE ELIOT

The souls of women are so small,
That some believe they've none
    at all. SAMUEL BUTLER

If men knew how women pass the time when they are alone, they'd never marry. O'HENRY

Men have as exaggerated an idea of their rights as women have of their wrongs. E. W. HOWE

There is nothing women hate so much as to see men selfishly enjoying themselves without the solace of feminine society. KATHARINE TYNAN HINKSON

Men have a much better time of it than women: for one thing, they marry later; for another thing they die earlier. H. L. MENCKEN

They exchanged the quick, brilliant smile of women who dislike each other on sight. MARSHALL PUGH

On one issue at least, men and women agree; they both distrust women. H. L. MENCKEN

Women, when they have made a sheep of a man, always tell him that he is a lion with a will of iron. HONORÉ DE BALZAC

What passes for women's intuition is often nothing more than man's transparency. GEORGE JEAN NATHAN

Women's styles may change but their designs remain the same. ANON

Women represent the triumph of matter over mind, just as men represent the triumph of mind over morals. OSCAR WILDE

Wooing: He that would the daughter win,
        Must with the mother first begin. ENGLISH PROVERB

Words: If it takes a lot of words to say what you have in mind, give it more thought. DENNIS ROCH

Work: The reason why worry kills more people than work is that more people worry than work. ROBERT FROST

My father taught me to work; he did not teach me to love it. ABRAHAM LINCOLN

I would rather make my name than inherit it. W. M. THACKERAY

It appears on close examination, that work is less boring than amusing oneself. CHARLES BAUDELAIRE

Worldliness: The knowledge of the world is only to be acquired in the world, and not in a closet. LORD CHESTERFIELD

Worry: If I spent as much time doing the things I worry about getting done, as I do worrying about doing them, I wouldn't have anything to worry about. ANON

Worry is interest paid on trouble before it falls due. DEAN W. R. INGE

Writer: Talent alone cannot make a writer. There must be a man behind the book. RALPH WALDO EMERSON

No one who cannot halt at self-imposed boundaries could ever write. NICOLAS BOILEAU

The greatest part of a writer's time is spent in reading, in order to write; a man will turn over half a library to make one book. SAMUEL JOHNSON

To write: that is to sit in judgement over one's self. IBSEN

The best way to become associated with a subject is to write a book about it. BENJAMIN DISRAELI

One man is as good as another until he has written a book. BENJAMIN JOWETT

One should always aim at being interesting rather than exact. VOLTAIRE

What is written without effort is in general read without pleasure. SAMUEL JOHNSON

When you take stuff from one writer it's plagiarism; but when you take it from many writers, it's research. WILSON MIZNER

The man who writes about himself and his own time is the only man who writes about all people and about all time. GEORGE BERNARD SHAW

Reading is not a duty, and has consequently no business to be made disagreeable. AUGUSTINE BIRRELL

In literature the ambition of the novice is to acquire the literary language; the struggle of the adept is to get rid of it. GEORGE BERNARD SHAW

How vain it is to sit down and write when you have not stood up to live. HENRY DAVID THOREAU

No great writer uses his skill to conceal his meaning. GEORGE BERNARD SHAW

All good books are alike in that they are truer than if they had really happened. ERNEST HEMINGWAY

The only sensible ends of literature are, first, the pleasurable toil of writing; second, the gratification of one's family and friends; and lastly the solid cash. NATHANIEL HAWTHORNE

Yourself: Never try to make anyone like yourself. You know, and God knows, that one of you is enough. ANON

Youth: The arrogance of age must submit to be taught by youth. EDMUND BURKE

I do beseech you to direct your efforts more to preparing youth for the path and less to preparing the path for youth. JUDGE BEN LINDSAY

Nobody can be so amusingly arrogant as a young man who has just discovered an old idea and thinks it is his own. SYDNEY HARRIS

Young men are apt to think themselves wise enough, as drunken men are apt to think themselves sober enough. LORD CHESTERFIELD